KT-416-471

 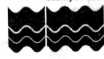

In This Book

QuickStart Guide

Your keys to understanding the city – we help you decide what to do and how to do it

Need to Know
Tips for a smooth trip

Neighbourhoods
What's where

Explore Prague

The best things to see and do, neighbourhood by neighbourhood

Top Sights
Make the most of your visit

Local Life
The insider's city

The Best of Prague

The city's highlights in handy lists to help you plan

Best Walks
See the city on foot

Prague's Best...
The best experiences

Survival Guide

Tips and tricks for a seamless, hassle-free city experience

Getting Around
Travel like a local

Essential Information
Including where to stay

Our selection of the city's best places to eat, drink and experience:

◉ **Sights**

✖ **Eating**

🚇 **Drinking**

★ **Entertainment**

🔒 **Shopping**

These symbols give you the vital information for each listing:

- ☎ Telephone Numbers
- ☺ Opening Hours
- 🅿 Parking
- ⊖ Nonsmoking
- @ Internet Access
- 📶 Wi-Fi Access
- ✒ Vegetarian Selection
- 📖 English-Language Menu
- 👪 Family-Friendly
- 🐾 Pet-Friendly
- 🚌 Bus
- 🚢 Ferry
- Ⓜ Metro
- Ⓢ Subway
- ⊖ London Tube
- 🚊 Tram
- 🚆 Train

Find each listing quickly on maps for each neighbourhood:

Bar Hemingway

16 🚇 Map p233, B2

Legend has it that Hemi self, wielding a machine rate this timber-pan ered bar during showpiece is a en by Papa ar town. Dress s.com; Hôtel Rit ☺6.30pm-2a

Plac

Lonely Planet's Prague

Lonely Planet Pocket Guides are designed to get you straight to the heart of the city.

Inside you'll find all the must-see sights, plus tips to make your visit to each one really memorable. We've split the city into easy-to-navigate neighbourhoods and provided clear maps so you'll find your way around with ease. Our expert authors have searched out the best of the city: walks, food, nightlife and shopping, to name a few. Because you want to explore, our 'Local Life' pages will take you to some of the most exciting areas to experience the real Prague.

And of course you'll find all the practical tips you need for a smooth trip: itineraries for short visits, how to get around, and how much to tip the guy who serves you a drink at the end of a long day's exploration.

It's your guarantee of a really great experience.

Our Promise

You can trust our travel information because Lonely Planet authors visit the places we write about, each and every edition. We never accept freebies for positive coverage, so you can rely on us to tell it like it is.

QuickStart Guide 7

Explore Prague 21

Worth a Trip:

The Best of Prague 129

Prague's Best Walks

Prague's Best ...

Survival Guide 145

QuickStart Guide

Welcome to Prague

More than 25 years after the Velvet Revolution drew back the curtain on this intoxicating maze of winding cobblestone alleyways, the 'city of a hundred spires' thrills visitors with dramatic Gothic architecture, down-to-earth pubs, fin de siè-cle cafes, cutting-edge art and the majestic Prague Castle – the world's largest – looming high over the Czech capital.

Astronomical Clock and Church of Our Lady Before Týn (p71), Prague's Old Town Square
LUCIANO MORTULA - LGM/SHUTTERSTOCK ©

Prague
Top Sights

Prague Castle (p24)
The Czech capital's top
sight.

St Vitus Cathedral
(p30) Prague Castle's
sky-piercing Gothic
centrepiece.

Old Town Square & Astronomical Clock

(p70) Historical square with its Astronomical Clock.

Charles Bridge

(p72) Stunning stone bridge spanning the Vltava.

Jewish Museum (p56)

Occupies six former Jewish sites.

Old Jewish Cemetery (p58)

Tiny cemetery with 12,000 tombstones.

Loreta (p32)

A baroque place of pilgrimage.

Petřín Hill (p40)
A 318m-high grassy city-centre knoll.

Wenceslas Square (p86)
Large, commercial and epicentral square.

Veletržní Palác (p120)
Impressive collection of avant-garde art.

Prague
Local Life

Local experiences and hidden gems
to help you uncover the real city

Czechs are a cool, laid-back bunch fond of walking their dogs down to the beer garden. After you've seen the castle and walked across Charles Bridge, join the locals in their favourite parks, residential neighbourhoods and watering holes.

Gardens of Malá Strana (p42)

☑ Inviting urban oases ☑ Picnic time

Drinking Tour of Vinohrady & Žižkov (p108)

☑ Funky nightlife ☑ Fashionable bars

Vyšehrad, Prague's Other Castle (p104)
☑ Ancient fortress and cemetery ☑ River and castle views

Other places to experience the city like a local:

Beer & Culture in Smíchov (p52)
☑ Edgy, alternative art ☑ Down-to-earth bars

Prague
Day Planner

Day One

Just one day in Prague? Focus on major sights. Start early, joining the crowd below the **Astronomical Clock** (p71) for the hourly chiming, then wander through the **Old Town Square** (p70), taking in the spectacular array of architectural styles and the spires of the **Church of Our Lady Before Týn** (p71). Stop for coffee and a bite at charming **Bakeshop Praha** (p63) before a short stroll through **Josefov** (p54), the former Jewish ghetto. You won't have time to see the **Prague Jewish Museum** (p56), but a walk will give you a feel for the place.

Amble through the winding alleys of the Old Town on your way to one of Prague's most famous landmarks, **Charles Bridge** (p72). While crossing the statue-decked bridge, stop to take photos of the Vltava River, with magnificent **Prague Castle** (p24) rising high over the historical cityscape. Hike up to the castle along **Nerudova** (p47) through Malá Strana and spend the afternoon visiting **St Vitus Cathedral** (p30) and the castle's gardens.

For dinner, treat yourself to a meal with a view at **Villa Richter** (p36), just near the castle, or walk back down to Malá Strana for upscale Czech food at **Augustine** (p48).

Day Two

Spend the morning exploring the quaint backstreets and **Kampa gardens** (p43) of Malá Strana, one of the city's oldest districts. Catch the **Petřín Funicular** (p41) to enjoy sweeping views from the **Lookout Tower** (p41) at the top of Petřín. From here, find the serene path that crosses over to the **Strahov Monastery** (p35), and then head downhill along **Nerudova** (p47), stopping into elegant **Wallenstein Garden** (p43) at the bottom. Laugh at the **Proudy** (p43) sculpture before treating yourself to a late lunch at the lovely riverside restaurant **Hergetova Cihelná** (p48).

Cross the river via Mánes Bridge. In the afternoon, check out the famous synagogues of the **Jewish Museum** (p56), and then take a break with coffee and cake on the balcony of the striking, cubist **Grand Cafe Orient** (p79).

Stop by the box office of the **National Theatre** (p101) to see if any last-minute tickets are available to the opera or ballet. Before the show, have a light meal at **Cafe Louvre** (p101). Afterwards, go for a classy nightcap at **Hemingway Bar** (p80) or **Tretter's New York Bar** (p64).

Short on time?
We've arranged Prague's must-sees into these day-by-day itineraries to make sure you see the very best of the city in the time you have available.

Day Three

☀ Start with coffee at the famous **Kavárna Slavia** (p101), choosing a table at the front looking across the river to Prague Castle. Amble over to **Slav Island** (p99) and rent a paddleboat to splash about in the river before heading south to see the **Dancing House** (p99). From here, walk back up Národní třída to **Wenceslas Square** (p86), taking time to see the nearby sights, including the **National Museum** (p91; under renovation), the **Jan Palach Memorial** (p87) and **St Wenceslas Statue** (p87). Plan lunch at **Room** (p90), for tapas, or **Jáma** (p92), for beer and burgers.

☀ From here it's an easy metro jaunt to Vyšehrad and the **Vyšehrad Citadel** (p104), where you can wander around the ruins and visit the graves of Dvořak and Mucha in the **cemetery** (p105), as well as admiring the views of the Vltava and Prague Castle.

☾ Head back towards town and spend the evening in Vinohrady and Žižkov, choosing one of the area's excellent restaurants, such as **Aromi** (p113) or **Kofein** (p114) – or simply go for a beer at the **Riegrovy Sady Beer Garden** (p109).

Day Four

☀ It's time to see a different part of Prague. Start on Old Town Sq and walk down elegant **Pařížská** (p144), before crossing Čech Bridge (Čechův most) and making the climb to **Letná Gardens** (p123). Admire the views from the top, and then make your way east to the **Letná Beer Garden** (p125) – if it's too early for beer, make a note to come back.

☀ It's a short walk to the **National Technical Museum** (p123) – perfect if you've got kids. Have lunch at **Kumbal** (p126), then visit Prague's best (and most underrated) art museum, **Veletržní Palác** (p120). If you've still got some energy (and daylight), stroll through **Stromovka Park** (p124) and enjoy Prague's prettiest piece of green.

☾ Head back towards the Letná beer garden to relax with a half-litre or two, then make your way back down towards town. Enjoy a meal at high-end **Kalina** (p77), then go for jazz at a nearby club like **Reduta** (p102) or the **AghaRTA Jazz Centrum** (p80). For a quieter option, head for the rooftop terrace **U Prince** (p77) to lift a glass to this lovely city on your last night in the Czech capital.

Need to Know

For more information, see Survival Guide (p145)

Currency
Czech crown (Koruna česká; Kč)

Language
Czech

Visas
Generally not required for stays of up to three months.

Money
ATMs are widely available and credit cards are accepted at many restaurants and hotels across the city.

Mobile Phones
The Czech Republic uses GSM 900, compatible with mobile phones from the rest of Europe, Australia and New Zealand (but not with most North American phones).

Time
Central European Time (GMT plus one hour)

Tipping
It's standard practice in pubs, cafes, restaurants and taxis to round up the bill to the nearest 50 or 100Kč if service has been good.

 **Before You Go**

Your Daily Budget

Budget less than €80
▶ Dorm beds €10–€20
▶ Excellent supermarkets for self-catering
▶ Admission to major tourist attractions €10

Midrange €80–€150
▶ Double room €120–160
▶ Three-course dinner in casual restaurant €30

Top end more than €150
▶ Double room or suite at luxury hotel €200–€260
▶ Seven-course tasting menu in top restaurant €90

Useful Websites

▶ **Lonely Planet** (www.lonelyplanet.com/czech-republic/prague) Destination info, hotel bookings, traveller forum and more.

▶ **Prague City Tourism** (www.prague.eu) Prague's official tourism portal.

▶ **Prague.com** (www.prague.com) A city guide plus hotel bookings.

▶ **Prague Public Transit** (www.dpp.cz) Handy journey planner for all public transport.

Advance Planning

Three months before Book accommodation if visiting in high season.

One month before Reserve tables at top-end restaurants, and buy tickets online for weekend visits to Karlštejn Castle.

One week before Make Friday- or Saturday-night reservations for any restaurants you don't want to miss. Check website programs for art galleries, jazz clubs and music venues.

② Arriving in Prague

Public transport and private taxis are easily available from both main arrival hubs.

✈ From Václav Havel Airport Prague

Destination	Best Transport
Old Town	Taxi or bus to metro station Nádraží Veleslavín, connection to Staroměstská metro station
Malá Strana & Hradčany	Taxi or bus 119 to metro station Nádraží Veleslavín, connection to Malostranská metro station
Wenceslas Sq	Airport Express (AE) bus to Hlavní Nádraží train station area
Vinohrady & Žižkov	Taxi or bus 119 to metro station Nádraží Veleslavín, connection to Náměstí Miru or Jiřího z Poděbrad metro station

🚆 From Praha Hlavní Nádraží Train Station

Destination	Best Transport
Old Town	Metro Line C to Muzeum, transfer to Line A to Staroměstská station
Malá Strana & Hradčany	Metro Line C to Muzeum, transfer to Line A to Malostranská station (plus tram for Hradčany)
Wenceslas Sq	Walk (it's two blocks away)
Vinohrady & Žižkov	Metro Line C to Muzeum, transfer to Line A to Náměstí Miru or Jiřího z Poděbrad metro station

③ Getting Around

Prague's public transport system is affordable and efficient, and one of Europe's best. Most visitors will get everywhere they need to by walking, taking the metro or hopping on a tram.

Ⓜ Metro

Prague's metro system runs from 5am to midnight, with fast, frequent service. For tourists, the most useful line is A (green), which runs from Nádraží Veleslavín (airport connection) to Prague Castle, Malá Strana, Old Town Sq, Wenceslas Sq and Vinohrady.

🚋 Tram

Travelling on the trams in Prague is part of the cultural experience. Regular trams run from 5am to midnight. Important lines to remember are 22 (runs to Prague Castle, Malá Strana and Charles Bridge, Nové Město, and Vinohrady), 17 and 18 (run to the Jewish Quarter and Old Town Sq) and 11 (runs to Žižkov and Vinohrady). After midnight, night trams (91 to 99) rumble across the city about every 40 minutes.

🚕 Taxi

Taxis are a convenient option when you're in a hurry, but be careful of scams. Look for the 'Taxi Fair Place' stations in key tourist areas: drivers can charge a maximum fare and must announce the estimated price in advance. Make sure you know the current exchange rate if the driver offers you the chance to pay in a foreign currency.

Prague Neighbourhoods

Jewish Museum & Josefov (p54)

Today, Prague's one-time Jewish ghetto is home to a cluster of historic synagogues and the eerie but beautiful Old Jewish Cemetery.

⊙ Top Sights

Jewish Museum

Old Jewish Cemetery

Prague Castle & Hradčany (p22)

This refined hilltop district is defined by the massive castle complex that gives Prague its dreamy, fairy-tale-like appearance.

⊙ Top Sights

Prague Castle

St Vitus Cathedral

Loreta

Malá Strana & Petřín Hill (p38)

Quaint, cobblestoned streets, red roofs, ancient cloisters and a peaceful hillside park characterise Prague's charming 'Lesser Quarter'.

⊙ Top Sights

Petřín Hill

Old Town Square & Staré Město (p68)

Gothic spires, art nouveau architecture, a quirky astronomical clock and horse-drawn carriages crowd this colourful, famous old square.

⊙ Top Sights

Old Town Square & Astronomical Clock

Charles Bridge

Wenceslas Square & Around (p84)

Once a horse market, this huge square has been the site of many important moments in Czech history.

⊙ Top Sights

Wenceslas Square

St Vitus Cathedral ⊙

Prague Castle ⊙

Loreta ⊙

Petřín Hill ⊙

Old Jewish Cemetery ⊙

Jewish Museum ⊙

Charles Bridge ⊙

Old Town Square & Astronomical Clock ⊙

◉
*Veletržní
Palác*

Holešovice (p118)
Beer gardens, contemporary art and huge parks characterise this laid-back district that's well off the tourist path.

◉ Top Sights
Veletržní Palác

◉
*Wenceslas
Square*

Nové Město (p96)
Cool modern architecture and quiet riverside cafes are the crowning glories of this underrated neighbourhood.

Vinohrady & Žižkov (p106)
The locals' residential neighbourhood of choice, this leafy area contains many of Prague's hippest bars and cafes.

Explore
Prague

Worth a Trip

View of Charles Bridge (p72)
S-F/SHUTTERSTOCK ©

Explore

Prague Castle & Hradčany

The spires of St Vitus Cathedral, rising up from the heart of Prague Castle, are rarely out of view when you're wandering around the city. In Hradčany (the castle district), visitors are particularly conscious of the royal omnipresence; passing through the doll-sized alleyways, you'll have an idea of what life was like for the castle's hard-working medieval minions.

The Sights in a Day

Get an early start for your assault on **Prague Castle**. Eat breakfast and have coffee beforehand, since there aren't many early-morning options up here. Buy an admission ticket at the information centre and head straight for **St Vitus Cathedral** (p30) to check out the magnificent church before the crowds show up. Visit the **Old Royal Palace** and **Golden Lane** before taking a break in the **Royal Garden**. Make your way back to the castle entrance for the changing of the guard at noon.

After lunch, walk down to the **Loreta** (p32) and take the audio tour of the major sights, including **Santa Casa** and the **Church of the Nativity of Our Lord**. Spend the rest of the afternoon perusing the National Gallery's fine holdings of European art at **Šternberg Palace** (p36) or the Theology and Philosophy halls of the nearly thousand-year-old **Strahov Monastery** (p35). Check out the nearby quirky **Miniature Museum** (p35).

Hradčany is quiet at night, but you can pair a late-afternoon stroll through the **Nový Svět quarter** (p36) with a romantic dinner at **U Zlaté Hrušky** (p36), or have something even more elegant at **Villa Richter** (p36).

Top Sights
Prague Castle (p24)

St Vitus Cathedral (p30)

Loreta (p32)

Best of Prague
Food
U Zlaté Hrušky (p36)

Villa Richter (p36)

Lobkowicz Palace Café (p36)

Art
Prague Castle Picture Gallery (p25)

Šternberg Palace (p36)

Stained-Glass Windows of St Vitus Cathedral (p31)

For Free
Prague Castle (p24)

Nový Svět Quarter (p36)

History
Tomb of St John of Nepomuk (p31)

Prague Sun (p33)

Strahov Monastery (p35)

Getting There

Ⓜ **Metro** Take Line A to Malostranská, then climb the steps.

🚊 **Tram** Take 22 to Pražský hrad then walk five minutes, or to Pohořelec then walk downhill.

Top Sights
Prague Castle

Known simply as *hrad* (castle) to proud Praguers, Prague Castle was founded by 9th-century Přemysl princes and grew haphazardly as subsequent rulers built additions. Today, it's a huge complex (larger than seven football fields) proceeding west to east through a series of three courtyards. There have been four major reconstructions. Many Czech rulers have resided here; one notable exception is the first postcommunist president, Václav Havel: in 1989, he plumped for the comforts of his own home instead.

⊙ Map p34, D2

www.hrad.cz

Hradčanské náměstí 1

grounds free, sights adult/concession Tour A & C 350/175Kc, Tour B 250/125Kc

⊘ grounds 6am-11pm year-round, gardens 10am-6pm Apr-Oct

Ⓜ Malostranská, 🚊22

Prague Castle's main gate

Castle Entrance

The castle's main gate, on Hradčany Sq, is flanked by huge, 18th-century statues of battling Titans that dwarf the castle guards below. Playwright-turned-president Václav Havel hired the Czech costume designer on the film *Amadeus* to redesign the guards' uniforms and instigated a changing-of-the-guard ceremony – the most impressive display is at noon.

Prague Castle Picture Gallery

In 1648 an invading Swedish army looted Emperor Rudolf II's art collection (as well as making off with the original bronze statues in the Wallenstein Garden). The **gallery** (adult/child 100/50Kč, admission incl with Prague Castle Tour C ticket; ⏱9am-5pm Apr-Oct, to 4pm Nov-Mar; 🚌22) in these converted Renaissance stables displays what was left, as well as replacement works, including some by Rubens, Tintoretto and Titian.

Plečnik Monolith

In the third courtyard, a noteworthy feature near St Vitus Cathedral is a huge granite monolith dedicated to the victims of WWI, designed by Slovene architect Jože Plečnik in 1928. Nearby is a copy of the castle's famous statue of St George slaying the dragon.

Old Royal Palace

The palace's highlight is the high-Gothic vaulted roof ofVladislav Hall (Vladislavský sál; 1493–1502), beneath which all the presidents of the Czech Republic have been sworn in. There's also a balcony off the hall with great city views and a door to the former Bohemian Chancellery, where the Second Defenestration of Prague occurred in 1618.

☑ Top Tips

▶ The castle buildings open at 9am; be there a few minutes early to beat the crowds.

▶ You'll need at least half a day to explore the castle grounds.

▶ Guided tours of the castle in English can be arranged in advance by calling ☎224 373 584. Tours last around an hour and leave from the information centres.

▶ To catch music and cultural events at the castle grounds, check out www.kulturanahrade. cz for a schedule of events.

✕ Take a Break

There are several places scattered around the castle grounds to stop for a coffee or cold drink. Our favourite – also good for lunch – is the lovely Lobkowicz Palace Café (p36), located on the ground level of Lobkowicz Palace.

Story of Prague Castle

One of the castle's most compelling exhibitions, with an outstanding collection of armour, jewellery, glassware, furniture and other artefacts from more than a thousand years of the castle's history. A particularly memorable sight is the skeleton of the pre-Christian 'warrior', still encased in the earth where archaeologists found him within the castle grounds.

Basilica of St George

Behind a brick-red facade lies the Czech Republic's best-preserved Romanesque church. The original was established in the 10th century by Vratislav I (the father of St Wenceslas), who is still buried here, as is St Ludmilla. It's also popular for small concert performances.

Golden Lane

The tiny, colourful cottages along this cobbled alley, reopened a couple of years ago after extensive renovations, were built in the 16th century for the castle guard's sharpshooters, but were later used by goldsmiths, squatters and artists, including writer Franz Kafka (who stayed at his sister's house at No 22 from 1916 to 1917).

Rosenberg Palace

Originally built as the grand residence of the Rosenberg family, this 16th-century Renaissance-style palace was later repurposed by Empress Maria Theresa as a 'Residence for Noblewomen' to house 30 unmarried women at a time. Today, one section of the palace recreates the style of an 18th-century noblewoman's apartment using artefacts from the Prague Castle's depository.

Lobkowicz Palace

The 16th-century **Lobkowicz Palace** (Lobkovický palác; ☎233 312 925; www. lobkowicz.com; Jiřská 3; adult/concession/family 275/200/690Kč; ⊙10am-6pm; 🚋22) houses a private museum known as the Princely Collections, with priceless paintings, furniture and musical memorabilia. An included audioguide dictated by owner William Lobkowicz and his family brings the displays to life, making this one of the castle's most interesting attractions.

Royal Garden

Powder Bridge (Prašný most; 1540) spans the Stag Moat (Jelení příkop) en route to the spacious Renaissance-style Royal Garden, dating from 1534. The most beautiful building is the Ball-Game House (Míčovna; 1569), a masterpiece of Renaissance sgraffito where the Habsburgs once played badminton. East is the Summer Palace (Letohrádek; 1538–60) and west the former Riding School (Jízdárna; 1695).

Southern Gardens

The three gardens lined up below the castle's southern wall – **Paradise Garden**, the **Hartig Garden** and the **Garden on the Ramparts** – offer superb views over Malá Strana's rooftops. Enter from the west via the New Castle Steps or from the east via the Old Castle Steps.

Understand
Kings & Castles

Prague's history, filled with royal betrayals, people tossing each other out of windows, and one man famously being burnt at the stake, makes *The Tudors* look tame by comparison.

In the Beginning
The name 'Bohemia', still used to describe the Czech Republic's western half, comes from a Celtic tribe, the Boii, who lived here for centuries before Slavic tribes arrived around the 6th century. The 9th-century Přemysl dynasty built the earliest section of today's Prague Castle in the 9th century, and also included one Václav, or 'Wenceslas', of 'Good King' Christmas-carol fame.

The Good Times
After the Přemysl dynasty died out, Prague came under the control of the family that eventually produced Holy Roman Emperor Charles IV (1316–78). Under his rule, the city blossomed. Charles, whose mother was Czech, elevated Prague's official status and went on a construction spree, building the New Town (Nové Město) and Charles Bridge, founding Charles University and adding St Vitus Cathedral to the castle.

University rector Jan Hus led the 15th-century Hussite movement, which challenged what many saw as the corrupt practices of the Catholic Church. Hus was burnt at the stake at Constance in 1415 for 'heresy' – this kicked off decades of sectarian fighting.

Habsburg Rule
In 1526 the Czech lands came under the rule of the Austrian Habsburgs. With the Reformation in full swing in Europe, tensions between the Catholic Habsburgs and reformist Czechs inevitably surfaced. In 1618, Bohemian rebels threw two Catholic councillors from a Prague Castle window, sparking the Thirty Years' War (1618–48). Following the defeat of the Czech nobility in 1620 at the Battle of White Mountain (Bílá Hora), Czechs lost their independence to the Habsburgs for 300 years.

Prague Castle

Old Castle Steps

Lobkowicz Palace Café

Lobkowicz Palace

Rosenberg Palace

Stag Moat

Golden Lane

Royal Garden

Basilica of St George

St George's Square

Story of Prague Castle

Old Royal Palace

Southern Gardens

St Vitus Cathedral

Third Courtyard

Plečnik Monolith

Powder Bridge

Information Centre

New Castle Steps

Prague Castle Picture Gallery

Second Courtyard

Information Centre

First Courtyard

Castle Entrance

Hradčany Sq

Basilica of St George

Visiting Prague Castle

You can purchase two kinds of tickets (each valid for two days) that allow entry to different combinations of sights. Most short-term visitors opt for the Short Tour:

The **Short Tour** (adult/child/family 250/125/500Kč) includes St Vitus Cathedral, Old Royal Palace, Basilica of St George, Golden Lane and Daliborka.

The **Long Tour** (adult/child/family 350/175/700Kč) includes St Vitus Cathedral, Story of Prague Castle, Basilica of St George, Powder Tower, Golden Lane and Daliborka, Prague Castle Picture Gallery, Powder Tower and Rosenberg Palace.

Buy tickets at the information centres in the Second and Third Courtyards.

Top Sights
St Vitus Cathedral

The largest and most noteworthy church in the Czech Republic was begun in 1344. Though it appears Gothic to the tips of its pointy spires, much of St Vitus Cathedral was only completed in time for its belated consecration in 1929. The coronations of Bohemia's kings were held here until the mid-19th century. Today it's the seat of the Archbishop of Prague and the final resting place of some of the nation's most illustrious figures – kings, princes, even saints.

👁 Map p34, D2

📞 257 531 622

www.katedralasvate
hovita.cz

Third Courtyard, Prague Castle

admission incl Prague Castle Tour A & B tickets

🕑9am-5pm Mon-Sat, noon-5pm Sun Apr-Oct, to 4pm Nov-Mar

🚊22

The cathedral's stained-glass windows

Stained-Glass Windows

The interior is flooded with colour from stained-glass windows created by eminent Czech artists of the early 20th century. In the third chapel on the northern side (to the left as you enter) is one by art nouveau artist Alfons Mucha, depicting the lives of Sts Cyril and Methodius.

Golden Gate

The cathedral's south entrance is known as the Golden Gate (Zlatá brána), an elegant, triple-arched Gothic porch designed by Peter Parler.

Royal Oratory

Kings addressed their subjects from this grand, intricately crafted oratory (1493) that appears to be woven with gnarled tree branches. This striking centrepiece exemplifies late-Gothic aesthetics.

Tomb of St John of Nepomuk

Nepomuk was a priest and a religious martyr; it's said that hundreds of years after his death, when his body was exhumed, his tongue was found 'still alive'. The Church canonised him and commissioned this elaborate silver sarcophagus for his reburial. (Scientists later showed that the 'tongue' was actually brain tissue congealed in blood.)

Chapel of St Wenceslas

This is the most beautiful of the cathedral's side chapels, with walls adorned with gilded panels containing polished slabs of semiprecious stones. Murals from the early 16th century depict scenes from the life of the Czechs' patron saint, while even older frescos show scenes from the life of Jesus. On the southern side a small door – locked with seven locks – leads to the coronation chamber, where the Bohemian crown jewels are kept.

☑ Top Tips

▶ Try to arrive first thing in the morning, when the crowds are smaller.

▶ Entry to the cathedral is included in both short- and long-term Prague Castle combined-entry tickets.

▶ For spectacular views, climb the stairway to the cathedral's tower.

✗ Take a Break

Before braving the crowds, fortify with a steaming cup of jasmine tea or light meal at Malý Buddha (p37), located outside the castle complex a short walk from the main entrance.

Top Sights
Loreta

The Loreta is a baroque place of pilgrimage financed by the noble Lobkowicz family in 1626. It was designed as a replica of the supposed Santa Casa (Sacred House, the home of the Virgin Mary) in the Holy Land. Legend has it that the original Santa Casa was carried by angels to the Italian town of Loreto as the Turks were advancing on Nazareth. The Loreta's original purpose was to wow and woo the local population, and it still manages to dazzle.

👁 Map p34, B3

☏ 220 516 740

www.loreta.cz

Loretánské náměstí 7

adult/child/family 150/80/310Kč, photography permit 100Kč

🕙 9am-5pm Apr-Oct, 9.30am-4pm Nov-Mar

🚋 22

Santa Casa

The duplicate Santa Casa is in the centre of a courtyard complex, surrounded by cloistered arcades, churches and chapels. The interior is adorned with 17th-century frescos and reliefs depicting the life of the Virgin Mary, and an ornate silver altar with a wooden effigy of Our Lady of Loreto.

Prague Sun

The eye-popping treasury boasts a star attraction – a dazzling object called the 'Prague Sun'. Studded with 6222 diamonds, it was a gift to the Loreta from Countess Ludmila of Kolowrat. In her will she wrote that the piece must be crafted from her personal collection of diamonds – wedding gifts from her third husband.

Church of the Nativity of Our Lord

Behind the Santa Casa is the Church of the Nativity of Our Lord, built in 1737 to a design by Christoph Dientzenhofer. The claustrophobic interior includes two skeletons of the Spanish saints Felicissima and Marcia, dressed in aristocratic clothing with wax masks concealing their skulls.

The Bearded Lady

At the corner of the courtyard is the unusual Chapel of Our Lady of Sorrows, featuring a crucified bearded lady. She was St Starosta, pious daughter of a Portuguese king who promised her to the king of Sicily against her wishes. After a night of tearful prayers she awoke with a beard, the wedding was called off, and her father had her crucified. She was later made patron saint of the needy and the god-forsaken.

☑ Top Tips

▶ The worthwhile audioguide, available in several languages, costs 150Kč.

▶ Families (two adults and up to five children under 16) can ask for the 310Kč family rate.

▶ If you'd like to take photos (no flash or tripod allowed), ask for a permit (100Kč).

✗ Take a Break

For a cold beer, look no further than old-school Czech pub Pivnice U Černého Vola (p37).

For something more substantial, like lunch or dinner, try the nearby U Zlaté Hrušky (p36). In summer, sit in the garden across the street.

200 m
0.1 miles

Royal Garden (Královská zahrada)

Stag Moat (Jelení příkop)

Golden Lane (Zlatá ulička) 5

Brusnice

George St (Jiřská) 6

St George Square (Jiřské náměstí)

Prague Castle

St Vitus Cathedral

Third Courtyard

Garden on the Ramparts (Zahrada Na Valech)

Castle Steps (Zámecké schody)

Second Courtyard

First Courtyard

Hradčany Square (Hradčanské náměstí)

U Prašného mostu

Šternberg Palace

Garden on the Bastion (Zahrada Na Baště) 3

HRADČANY

Mariánské hradby

Keplerova

U Brusnice

NOVÝ SVĚT

7

U Kasáren

Nový Svět Quarter

Nový Svět

Loretánská

Loreta

Kapucínská

Loreta Square (Loretánské náměstí)

9

11 8

Černínská

Černín Palace (Černínský palác)

Pohořelec

10 2 Miniature Museum

4

1 Strahov Monastery

Strahovská zahrada

Lobkovická zahrada

Schönbornská zahrada

Seminářská zahrada

Vrtbov Garden (Vrtbovská zahrada)

Malá Strana Square (Malostranské náměstí)

Mostecká

Tržiště

Vlašská

Jánský vršek

Nerudova

Ke Hrad

Úvoz

Thunovská

PRAHA 1

Sněmovní

Wallenstein Square (Valdštejnské náměstí)

Tomášská

Strahov Library

Sights

Strahov Monastery MONASTERY

1 ◎ Map p34, A4

In 1140 Vladislav II founded Strahov Monastery for the Premonstratensian order. The present monastery buildings, completed in the 17th and 18th centuries, functioned until the communist government closed them down and imprisoned most of the monks; they returned in 1990. The magnificent **Strahov Library** (Strahovská knihovna; 📞 233 107 718; adult/child 100/50Kč; ◷9am-noon & 1-5pm) is the main attraction here. (Strahovský klášter; 📞 233 107 711, guided tours 602 190 297; www.strahov skyklaster.cz; Strahovské nádvoří 1; 🚋22)

Miniature Museum MUSEUM

2 ◎ Map p34, A4

Siberian technician Anatoly Konyenko once manufactured tools for microsurgery, but in his spare time he spent 7½ years crafting a pair of golden horseshoes for a flea. See those, as well as the Lord's Prayer inscribed on a single human hair, a grasshoper clutching a violin, and a camel caravan silhouetted in the eye of a needle. Weird but fascinating. (Muzeum Miniatur; 📞 233 352 371; www.muzeumminiatur.cz; Strahovské nádvoří II; adult/child 100/50Kč; ◷10am-5pm; 🚋22)

Šternberg Palace

GALLERY

3 Map p34, C2

The baroque Šternberg Palace is home to the National Gallery's collection of European art, from ancient Greece and Rome up to the 18th century, including works by Goya and Rembrandt. Fans of medieval altarpieces will be in heaven; there are also several Rubens, some Brueghels, and a large collection of Bohemian miniatures. (Šternberský palác; ☏ 233 090 570; www.ngprague. cz; Hradčanské náměstí 15; incl admission to all National Gallery venues, adult/child 300/150Kč; ⏲ 10am-6pm Tue-Sun; ☒ 22)

Nový Svět Quarter

AREA

4 Map p34, B2

In the 16th century, houses were built for castle staff in an enclave of curving cobblestone streets down the slope north of the Loreta. Today these diminutive cottages have been restored and painted in pastel shades, making the 'New World' quarter a perfect alternative to the castle's crowded Golden Lane. Danish astronomer Tycho Brahe once lived at Nový Svět 1. (☒ 22)

Eating

Villa Richter

CZECH, FRENCH €€

5 Map p34, E2

Housed in a restored 18th-century villa in the middle of a replanted medieval vineyard, this place is aimed squarely at the hordes of tourists

thronging up and down the Old Castle Steps. But the setting is special – outdoor tables on terraces with one of the finest views in the city – and the menu of classic Czech dishes doesn't disappoint. (☏ 702 205 108; www.villarichter.cz; Staré zamecké schody 6; mains 150-300Kč; 3-course dinner 945Kč; ⏲ 11am-11pm Mar-Oct; Ⓜ Malostranská)

Lobkowicz Palace Café

CAFE €€

6 Map p34, E2

This cafe, housed in the 16th-century Lobkowicz Palace, is the best eatery in the castle complex by an imperial mile. Try to grab one of the tables on the balconies at the back – the view over the city is superb, as is the goulash. The coffee is good too, and service is fast and friendly. (☏ 233 312 925; Jiřská 3; mains 200-300Kč; ⏲ 10am-6pm; 🛜 🚻; ☒ 22)

U Zlaté Hrušky

CZECH €€

7 Map p34, B2

'At the Golden Pear' is a cosy, wood-panelled gourmets' corner, serving Bohemian fish, fowl and game dishes and frequented by locals and visiting dignitaries as well as tourists (the Czech foreign ministry is just up the road, and Margaret Thatcher once dined here). In summer get a table in its leafy *zahradní restaurace* (garden restaurant) across the street. (☏ 220 941 244; www.restaurantuzlatehrusky.cz; Nový Svět 3; mains 390-490Kč; ⏲ 11am-1am; ☒ 22)

Malý Buddha

ASIAN €

8 ✕ Map p34, A3

Candlelight, incense and a Buddhist shrine characterise this intimate, vaulted restaurant that tries to capture the atmosphere of an oriental tearoom. The menu is a mix of Asian influences, with authentic Thai, Chinese and Vietnamese dishes, many of them vegetarian, and a drinks list that includes ginseng wine, Chinese rose liqueur and all kinds of tea. Credit cards are not accepted. (☎220 513 894; www.malybuddha.cz; Úvoz 46; mains 100-300Kč; ⊗noon-10.30pm Tue-Sun; ✏; ☒22)

Drinking

Pivnice U Černého Vola

PUB

9 🚇 Map p34, B3

Many religious people make a pilgrimage to the Loreta, but just across the road, the 'Black Ox' is a shrine that pulls in pilgrims of a different kind. This surprisingly inexpensive beer hall is visited by real-ale aficionados for its authentic atmosphere and lip-smackingly delicious draught beer, Velkopopovický Kozel (31Kč for 0.5L), brewed in a small town southeast of Prague. (☎220 513 481; Loretánské náměstí 1; ⊗10am-10pm; ☒22)

Klášterní Pivovar Strahov

BREWERY

10 🚇 Map p34, A4

Dominated by two polished copper brewing kettles, this convivial little pub in Strahov Monastery serves up two varieties of its St Norbert beer – *tmavý* (dark), a rich, tarry brew with a creamy head, and *polotmavý* (amber), a full-bodied, hoppy lager; both cost 65Kč per 0.4L. There's also a strong (6.3% alcohol) IPA-style beer. (Strahov Monastery Brewery; ☎233 353 155; www.klasterni-pivovar.cz; Strahovské nádvoří 301; ⊗10am-10pm; ☒22)

Shopping

Houpací Kůň

TOYS

11 🔒 Map p34, A3

The 'Rocking Horse' toy shop houses a collection of wooden folk dolls, 1950s wind-up tractors, toy cars and – surprise – even a couple of rocking horses. There are quality toys and art supplies you won't find anywhere else in Prague, but for a typically Czech souvenir try the famous and ubiquitous Little Mole cartoon character, available here in several guises. (☎603 515 745; Loretánské náměstí 3; ⊗9.30am-6.30pm; ☒22)

Explore

Malá Strana & Petřín Hill

Almost too picturesque for its own good, the baroque district of Malá Strana (Little Quarter) tumbles down the hillside between Prague Castle and the river. The focal point here is Malostranské náměstí, the main square, dominated by the green dome of St Nicholas Church. Petřín Hill, topped by a park and faux-but-fun Eiffel Tower, rises south of the square.

The Sights in a Day

Start your day on **Malostranské náměstí**; grab a coffee at the **Malostranská beseda** (p50) cafe to fortify yourself and admire the baroque splendour of **St Nicholas Church** (p45). Stroll the area's beautiful lanes and then stop by the **Karel Zeman Museum** (p46), **Kampa Museum** (p46) or the **Museum of the Infant Jesus of Prague** (p46) for some film, art or religious art. Grab lunch at **Cukrkávalimonáda** (p48).

After lunch, you've got an uphill choice. If you've got kids in tow, hike or (better yet) take the **Funicular** (p41) to Petřín Hill and its host of kid-friendly activities, including an impressive **Lookout Tower** (p41) and **Mirror Maze** (p41). Another option is to climb **Nerudova Street** (p47) starting from behind **Malostranské náměstí**, noting the characteristic medieval signs on the doors of the houses.

For the evening, dine riverside on the terrace of **Hergetova Cihelna** (p48) or go for something slightly higher-quality at **Augustine** (p48). Afterwards, take in some for jazz at **U Malého Glena** (p50) or catch a local band at **Malostranská beseda** (p50). For drinks, there's **Mlýnská Kavárna** (p50) or the ever-crazy **Blue Light** (p51).

For a local's day in Malá Strana see p42.

 Top Sights

Petřín Hill (p40)

Local Life

Gardens of Malá Strana (p42)

Best of Prague

Bars & Pubs
Blue Light (p51)

Mlýnská Kavárna (p50)

Food
Augustine (p48)

Café Savoy (p48)

Hergetova Cihelna (p48)

Museums
Franz Kafka Museum (p46)

Karel Zeman Museum (p46)

Museum of the Infant Jesus of Prague (p46)

Culture
U Malého Glena (p50)

Malostranská beseda (p50)

Getting There

Tram Take tram 12, 15, 20, 22 or 23 to Malostranské náměstí or to Újezd

M Metro The closest stop is Malostranská on Line A.

Top Sights
Petřín Hill

This 318m-high hill is one of Prague's largest green spaces. It's great for quiet, tree-shaded walks and fine views over the 'city of a hundred spires' from the observation deck of a highly convincing Eiffel Tower wannabe. There were once vineyards here, and a quarry that provided the stone for most of Prague's Romanesque and Gothic buildings. Take the funicular railway up to add a bit of a day-trip feel.

👁 Map p44, B3

🚋 Nebozízek, Petřín

Petřín Lookout Tower

Petřín Funicular

First opened in 1891, the **Petřín Funicular Railway** (Lanová draha na Petřín; ☏ 800 191 817; www.dpp.cz; Újezd; adult/child 32/16Kč; ☯ 9am-11.30pm; ☒ 9, 12, 15, 20, 22) trundles along 510m of track every 15 minutes from Újezd to the Petřín Lookout Tower, with a stop at Nebozízek.

Petřín Lookout Tower

Some of the best views of Prague – including, on a clear day, the Central Bohemian forests – are from the top of this 62m-tall **tower** (Petřínská rozhledna; ☏ 257 320 112; www.petrinska-rozhledna.cz; Petřínské sady; adult/child 120/65Kč; ☯ 10am-10pm Apr-Sep, to 8pm Mar & Oct, to 6pm Nov-Feb; ☒ Petřín), built in 1891 for the Prague Exposition. The Eiffel Tower lookalike has 299 steps (and a lift).

Memorial to the Victims of Communism

The striking **Memorial to the Victims of Communism** (Památník obětem komunismu; cnr Újezd & Vítězná; ☒ 9, 12, 15, 20, 22) sculpture shows disintegrating human figures descending a staggered slope. A bronze plaque records the terrible human toll of the communist era: 205,486 arrested; 170,938 driven into exile; 248 executed; 4500 who died in prison; and 327 shot trying to escape.

Mirror Maze

The **Mirror Maze** (Zrcadlové bludiště; www.petrinska-rozhledna.cz; Petřínské sady; adult/child 75/55Kč; ☯ 10am-10pm Apr-Sep, to 8pm Mar & Oct, to 6pm Nov-Feb; ☒ Petřín), just below the Lookout Tower, was also built for the 1891 Prague Exposition. The maze of distorting mirrors was based on the Prater in Vienna; there's also, inexplicably, a diorama of the 1648 Battle of Prague.

☑ Top Tips

▶ Before heading up the hill, stop at a bakery or supermarket to pick up picnic fare. There are lots of benches and places to unfurl a blanket.

▶ Hiking up Petřín Hill is a pleasant alternative to the funicular and not too strenuous if you follow the winding paths.

▶ Ride the funicular at night for glittering views out over the city.

▶ Instead of taking the funicular down, consider walking northward through the top of the park towards Strahov Monastery.

✗ Take a Break

Restaurant Nebozízek (☏ 257 315 329; www.nebozizek.cz; Petřínské sady 411; mains 150-420Kč; ☯ 11am-10pm; ☒ Nebozízek) is located halfway up Petřín Hill's funicular route – it offers wonderful views and is also accessible by foot.

Café Savoy (p48), not far from the funicular base station, is great for coffee or lunch.

Local Life
Gardens of Malá Strana

The aristocrats who inhabited Malá Strana in the 17th and 18th centuries sculpted beautiful baroque gardens, many of which are open to the public. From April to October, whenever the sun shines the neighbourhood's parks and gardens fill up with local students toting sketchbooks, young mothers with kids, and business types relaxing on their lunch breaks. Note that from November to March many of the parks are closed.

....

❶ **Stroll the Gardens Beneath Prague Castle**

The beautiful, terraced **Gardens Beneath Prague Castle** (Palácové zahrady pod Pražským hradem; ☎257 010 401; www.palacove-zahrady. cz; Valdštejnská 12-14; adult/child 90/60Kč; ⏱10am-7pm May-Sep, to 6pm Apr & Oct; Ⓜ Malostranská, ☐12, 15, 20, 22) on the steep southern slopes below the castle date

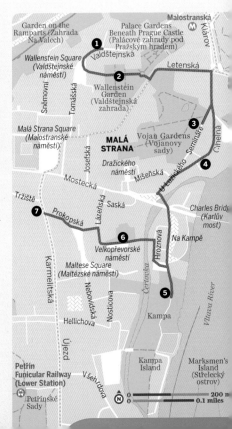

from the 17th and 18th centuries. They were restored in the 1990s and contain a Renaissance loggia with frescos of Pompeii and a baroque portal with sundial that cleverly catches the sunlight reflected off a fountain's water.

❷ Admire Wallenstein Garden

Baroque **Wallenstein Garden** (Valdštejnská zahrada; www.senat.cz; Letenská 10; admission free; ⏱7.30am-6pm Mon-Fri, 10am-6pm Sat & Sun Mar-Oct, to 7pm daily Jun-Sep; Ⓜ Malostranská, 🚋12, 15, 20, 22) is an oasis of peace amid the bustle of Malá Strana. Created for Duke Albrecht of Wallenstein in the 17th century, its finest feature is the huge loggia decorated with scenes from the Trojan Wars, flanked to one side by an enormous fake stalactite grotto dotted with carved grotesque faces.

❸ Hang Out With Locals in Vojan Gardens

While less manicured than most of Malá Strana's parks, **Vojan Gardens** (Vojanovy sady; U Lužického semináře; admission free; ⏱8am-dusk; Ⓜ Malostranská) is a popular spot with locals who like to come here to take a breather with the kids, sit in the sun or even hold summer parties.

❹ Spot an Unusual Fountain

In the open-air plaza in front of the Franz Kafka Museum is a much-photographed public artwork: David Černý's sculpture **Proudy** (Currents; www.david-cerny.cz; Hergetova Cihelná; Ⓜ Malostranská). The quirky animatronic sculpture features two men relieving themselves

into a puddle shaped like the Czech Republic. The microchip-controlled sculptures write out famous literary quotations of Prague with the streams.

❺ Feel the Breeze at Kampa

Toss a Frisbee, take a load off, or just watch the local hipsters play with their dogs at the leafy riverside park known simply as **Kampa** (🚋12, 15, 20, 22) (from the Latin *campus* or 'field'). One of the city's favourite chill-out zones, it's usually littered with lounging bodies – and excessively romantic teenagers – in summer.

❻ Find Inner Peace

The **John Lennon Wall** (Velkopřevorské náměstí; 🚋12, 15, 20, 22) is a memorial graffiti wall to the former Beatle. After his murder in New York in 1980, Lennon became a pacifist hero for young Czechs; his image was painted on this wall opposite the French Embassy, along with political graffiti and Beatles lyrics.

❼ Discover the Vrtbov Garden

The 'secret' **Vrtbov Garden** (Vrtbovská zahrada; ☎257 531 480; www.vrtbovska.cz; Karmelitská 25; adult/concession 65/55Kč; ⏱10am-6pm Apr-Oct; 🚋12, 15, 20, 22), hidden along an alley at the corner of Tržiště and Karmelitská, was built in 1720 for the Earl of Vrtba, the senior chancellor of Prague Castle. It's a formal baroque garden, climbing steeply up the hillside to a terrace graced with baroque statues of Roman mythological figures by Matthias Braun.

HRADČANY

Hradčany Square
(Hradčanské
náměstí)

U Kasáren

Loretánská

Ke Hra

Úvoz

Prague Castle
(Pražský hrad)

Garden on the Ramparts
(Zahrada Na Valech)

Thunovská

Nerudova

7

Jánský vršek

Šporkova

Vlašská

8

Quo Vadis (David
Černý Sculpture)

Schönbornská
zahrada

Lobkovická
zahrada

Petřín

Růžový
sady

Petřín Funicular Railway
(Upper Station)

Letenská

Klárov

Manes Bridge
(Mánesův
most)

Wallenstein Garden
(Valdštejnská
zahrada)

Tomášská

Sněmovní

MALÁ STRANA

10

Josefská

U Lužického semináře

Vojan Gardens
(Vojanovy
sady)

Franz Kafka
Museum

6

Cihelná

13

Charles Bridge
(Karlův most)

Vltava River

Malá Strana Square
(Malostranské náměstí)

18

22

2

St Nicholas Church
Bell Tower

St Nicholas
Church 1

Tržiště

Mostecká

Karmelitská

21

Vrtbov Garden
(Vrtbovská zahrada)

Museum of the
Infant Jesus 4
of Prague

Seminářská
zahrada

Petřín Funicular Railway
(Lower Station)

U Lanové
Dráhy

Petřínské
Sady

Nebozízek
Station

24   25

Míšeňská

Saská

Maltese
Square

9

17

Karel Zeman
Museum
3

Prokopská

Velkopřevorské
náměstí

Nebovidská

12

Hellichova

Harantova

23

Na Kampě

Kampa
Museum

5

U Sovových mlýnů

Kampa
Island

Čertovka

16

15

Všehrdova

Újezd

19

20

Říční

Vítězná

Legion Bridge

200 m
0.1 miles

St Nicholas Church

Sights

St Nicholas Church CHURCH

1 ⊙ Map p44, C2

Malá Strana is dominated by the huge green cupola of St Nicholas Church, one of Central Europe's finest baroque buildings. (Don't confuse it with the other Church of St Nicholas on Old Town Square.) On the ceiling, Johann Kracker's 1770 *Apotheosis of St Nicholas* is Europe's largest fresco (clever trompe l'oeil techniques have made the painting merge almost seamlessly with the architecture). (Kostel sv Mikuláše; ☏ 257 534 215; www.stnicholas.cz; Malostranské náměstí 38; adult/child 70/50Kč; ⊙ 9am-5pm Mar-Oct, to 4pm Nov-Feb; ☐ 12, 15, 20, 22)

St Nicholas Church Bell Tower TOWER

2 ⊙ Map p44, C2

During the communist era, the bell tower of St Nicholas Church was used to spy on the nearby American embassy – on the way up you can still see a small, white cast-iron urinal that was installed for the use of the watchers. Today it provides visitors with a grand view over Malá Strana and Charles Bridge. (http://en.muzeumprahy.cz/prague-towers; Malostranské náměstí; adult/child 90/65Kč; ⊙ 10am-10pm Apr-Sep, to 8pm Mar & Oct, to 6pm Nov-Feb; ☐ 12, 15, 20, 22)

Karel Zeman Museum
MUSEUM

3 ⊙ Map p44, D2

Bohemia-born director Karel Zeman (1910–89) was a pioneer of movie special effects whose work is little known outside the Czech Republic. This fascinating museum, established by his daughter, reveals the many tricks and techniques he perfected, and even allows visitors a bit of hands-on interaction – you can film yourself on your smartphone against painted backgrounds and 3D models. (Museum of Film Special Effects; ☎724 341 091; www.muzeumkarlazemana.cz; Saský dvůr, Saská 3; adult/child 200/140Kč; ⊙10am-7pm, last admission 6pm; ☒12, 15, 20, 22)

Museum of the Infant Jesus of Prague
MUSEUM

4 ⊙ Map p44, C3

The Church of Our Lady Victorious (kostel Panny Marie Vítězné), built in 1613, has on its central altar a 47cm-tall waxwork figure of the baby Jesus, brought from Spain in 1628 and known as the Infant Jesus of Prague (Pražské Jezulátko). At the back of the church is a museum, displaying a selection of the frocks used to dress the Infant. (Muzeum Pražského Jezulátka; ☎257 533 646; www.pragjesu.cz; Karmelitská 9; admission free; ⊙church 8.30am-7pm Mon-Sat, to 8pm Sun, museum 9.30am-5.30pm Mon-Sat, 1-6pm Sun, closed 1 Jan, 25 & 26 Dec & Easter Mon; ☒12, 15, 20, 22)

Kampa Museum
GALLERY

5 ⊙ Map p44, D3

Housed in a renovated mill building, this gallery is devoted to 20th-century and contemporary art from Central Europe. The highlights of the permanent exhibition are extensive collections of bronzes by cubist sculptor Otto Gutfreund and paintings by František Kupka; the most impressive canvas is Kupka's *Cathedral,* a pleated mass of blue-and-red diagonals. Outside you can get a close-up look at some of David Černý's famous crawling babies (the ones that swarm over the TV Tower (p112) in Žižkov). (Muzeum Kampa; ☎257 286 147; www.museumkampa.cz; U Sovových mlýnů 2; adult/concession 240/120Kč; ⊙10am-6pm; ☒12, 15, 20, 22)

Franz Kafka Museum
MUSEUM

6 ⊙ Map p44, E2

This much-hyped exhibition on the life and work of Prague's most famous literary son, entitled 'City of K', explores the intimate relationship between the writer and the city that shaped him, through the use of original letters, photographs, quotations, period newspapers and publications, and video and sound installations. (Muzeum Franze Kafky; ☎257 535 373; www.kafkamuseum.cz; Cihelná 2b; adult/child 200/120Kč; ⊙10am-6pm; Ⓜ Malostranská, ☒12, 15, 20, 22)

Understand
The Numbers Game

Until numbering was introduced in the 18th century, exotic house names and signs were the only way of identifying individual Prague buildings. This practice came to a halt in 1770, when it was banned by the city councillors.

More such-named houses and signs survive on **Nerudova** than along any other Prague street. As you head downhill look out for At the Two Suns (No 47), the Golden Horseshoe (No 34), the Three Fiddles (No 12), the Red Eagle (No 6) and the Devil (No 4). Other signs include a St Wenceslas on horseback (No 34), a golden key (No 27) and a golden goblet (No 16).

Nerudova STREET

 7 Map p44, B1

Following the tourist crowds downhill from the castle via Ke Hradu, you will arrive at Nerudova, architecturally the most important street in Malá Strana; most of its old Renaissance facades were 'baroquefied' in the 18th century. It's named after the Czech poet Jan Neruda (famous for his short stories, *Tales of Malá Strana*), who lived at the **House of the Two Suns** (dům U dvou slunců; Nerudova 47) from 1845 to 1857. (🚊12, 15, 20, 22)

Quo Vadis (David Černý Sculpture) MONUMENT

8 Map p44, B2

This golden Trabant (an East German car) on four human legs is a David Černý tribute to the 4000 East Germans who occupied the garden of the then West German embassy in 1989,

before being granted political asylum and leaving their Trabants behind. You can see the sculpture through the fence behind the German embassy. Head uphill along Vlašská, turn left into a children's park, and left again to find it. (Where Are You Going; www.david-cerny.cz; Vlašská 19; 🚊12, 15, 20, 22)

Maltese Square SQUARE

 9 Map p44, D2

References to the Knights of Malta around Malá Strana hark back to 1169, when the military order established a monastery in the Church of Our Lady Beneath the Chain on the square. Disbanded by the communists, the Knights have regained much property under post-1989 restitution laws, including the John Lennon Wall (p43). (Maltézské náměstí; 🚊12, 15, 20, 22)

Eating

Augustine
CZECH, EUROPEAN €€€

10 Map p44, D1

Hidden away in the historic Augustine Hotel (check out the ceiling fresco in the bar), this sophisticated yet relaxed restaurant is well worth seeking out. The menu ranges from down-to-earth but delicious dishes such as pork cheeks braised in the hotel's own St Thomas beer, to inventive dishes built around fresh Czech produce. The two-course business lunch costs 380Kč. (☏266 112 280; www.augustine-restaurant.cz; Letenská 12, Augustine Hotel; mains 350-590Kč, 4-course tasting menu 1350Kč; ⊙7am-11pm; ☏; ☐12, 15, 20, 22)

Café Savoy
EUROPEAN €€

11 Map p44, D4

The Savoy is a beautifully restored belle-époque cafe, with smart, suited waiting staff and a Viennese-style menu of hearty soups, salads, roast meats and schnitzels. There's also a 'gourmet menu' (mains 400Kč to 700Kč) where the star of the show is Parisian steak tartare mixed at your table, and a superb wine list (ask the staff for recommendations). (☏257 311 562; http://cafesavoy.ambi.cz; Vítězná 5; mains 200-400Kč; ⊙8am-10.30pm Mon-Fri, 9am-10.30pm Sat & Sun; ☏; ☐9, 12, 15, 20, 22)

U Modré Kachničky
CZECH €€€

12 Map p44, D3

A plush and chintzy 1930s-style hunting lodge hidden away on a quiet side street, 'At the Blue Duckling' is a pleasantly old-fashioned place with quiet, candlelit nooks perfect for a romantic dinner. The menu is heavy on traditional Bohemian duck and game dishes, such as roast duck with *slivovice* (plum brandy), plum sauce and potato pancakes. (☏257 320 308; www.umodrekachnicky.cz; Nebovidská 6; mains 475-600Kč; ⊙noon-4pm & 6.30pm-midnight; ☏; ☐12, 15, 20, 22)

Hergetova Cihelna
MEDITERRANEAN, ASIAN €€€

13 Map p44, E2

Housed in a converted 18th-century *cihelná* (brickworks), this place enjoys one of Prague's hottest locations, with a riverside terrace offering sweeping views of Charles Bridge. The menu is as sweeping as the view, ranging from fish and steak to Czech game dishes such as saddle of venison and wild boar ragout. There's also a decent kids menu and play area. (☏296 826 103; www.kampagroup.com; Cihelná 2b; mains lunch 200-400Kč, dinner 400-700Kč; ⊙11.30am-4pm & 6pm-1am; ☏ ☖; Ⓜ Malostranská)

Cukrkávalimonáda
EUROPEAN €

14 Map p44, D2

A cute little cafe-cum-restaurant that combines minimalist modern styling with Renaissance-era painted timber roof-beams, CKL offers fresh, home-made pastas, frittatas, ciabattas, salads and pancakes (sweet and savoury) by day and a slightly more sophisticated bistro menu in the early evening.

ANGYALOSI BEATA/SHUTTERSTOCK ©

Nerudova street (p47)

There's also a good breakfast menu offering ham and eggs, croissants, and yoghurt, and the hot chocolate is to die for. (☎257 225 396; www.cukrkavali-monada.com; Lázeňská 7; mains 100-200Kč; ☺9am-7pm; 🚊12, 15, 20, 22)

Bar Bar
CZECH, EUROPEAN €€

15 🍴 Map p44, D4

This friendly cellar bar is frequented more by locals than tourists, but the healthy-eating menu is chalked on a blackboard in both Czech and English. It ranges from braised beef cheeks with potato and chive mash, to roast trout with lime risotto, with a couple of good veggie alternatives. The weekday lunch menu offers soup and a main course for 156Kč. (☎257 312 246; www.bar-bar.cz; Všehrdova 17; mains 140-305Kč; ☺11am-11pm; 🖊; 🚊9, 12, 15, 20, 22)

Noi
THAI €€

16 🍴 Map p44, C4

A restaurant that feels more like a club, Noi is super-stylish with a chilled-out atmosphere and oriental design. The decor is based around lotus blossoms, lanterns and soft lighting, and the menu follows the Asian theme with competent Thai dishes such as chicken in red curry, and pad thai noodles, which – unusually for a Prague restaurant – has a hefty chilli kick. (☎257 311 411; www.noirestaurant.cz; Újezd 19; mains 210-325Kč; ☺11am-1am; 🛜; 🚊12, 15, 20, 22)

Café de Paris

FRENCH €€

17 Map p44, D2

A little corner of France tucked away on a quiet square, the Café de Paris is straightforward and unpretentious. So is the menu – onion soup or foie gras terrine to start, followed by entrecôte steak with chips, salad and a choice of sauces (they're very proud of the Café de Paris sauce, made to a 75-year-old recipe). (☑603 160 718; www.cafedeparis.cz; Maltézské náměstí 4; mains 245-470Kč; ⏱11.30am-midnight; ⛟12, 15, 20, 22)

Drinking

Malostranská Beseda

BAR, CLUB

18 Map p44, D1

Malá Strana's four-storey pleasure palace includes a fabled music club on the 2nd floor, with a lively roster of cabaret acts, jazz and old Czech rockers. There's also an art gallery on the top floor, a bar and restaurant on the ground floor, and a big beer hall in the basement serving Pilsner Urquell and Velkopopovický Kozel at 39Kč per 0.5L. (☑257 409 123; www.malostranska-beseda.cz; Malostranské náměstí 21; shows 120-250Kč; ⏱bar 4pm-1am, box office 5-9pm Mon-Sat, to 8pm Sun; ⛟12, 15, 20, 22)

Mlýnská Kavárna

BAR

19 Map p44, D4

This cafe-bar in Kampa park has existed in various guises since the communist era, and you might still hear it called Tato Kejkej, its previous incarnation, or just Mlýn (the mill). A wooden footbridge leads from Kampa to the smoky, dimly lit interior which is peopled with local artists (David Černý is a regular), writers and politicians. (☑257 313 222; Všehrdova 14; ⏱noon-midnight; 📶; ⛟9, 12, 15, 20, 22)

Klub Újezd

BAR

20 Map p44, D4

Klub Újezd is one of Prague's many 'alternative' bars, spread over three floors (DJs in the cellar, and a cafe upstairs) and filled with a fascinating collection of original art and weird wrought-iron sculptures. Clamber onto a two-tonne bar stool in the agreeably grungy street-level bar, and sip on a beer beneath a scaly, fire-breathing sea monster. (☑251 510 873; www.klubujezd.cz; Újezd 18; ⏱2pm-4am; ⛟9, 12, 15, 20, 22)

U Malého Glena

BAR

21 Map p44, C2

'Little Glen's' is a long-standing American-owned bar where hard-swinging local jazz or blues bands play every night in the cramped and steamy stone-vaulted cellar. There are Sunday-night jam sessions where amateurs are welcome (as long as you're good!) – it's a small venue, so get here early if you want to see as well as hear the band. (☑257 531 717; www.malyglen.cz; Karmelitská 23; ⏱10am-2am Sun-Thu, to 3am Fri & Sat, music from 8.30pm; 📶; ⛟12, 15, 20, 22)

Blue Light
COCKTAIL BAR

22 Map p44, D2

The Blue Light is a dark and atmospheric hang-out, as popular with locals as with tourists, where you can sip a caipirinha or cranberry colada as you cast an eye over the vintage jazz posters, records, old photographs and decades worth of scratched graffiti that adorn the walls. Often heaving on weekend nights. (☎257 533 126; www.bluelightbar.cz; Josefská 1; ⏰6pm-3am Mon-Fri, 7pm-3am Sat & Sun; 🚋12, 15, 20, 22)

Shopping

Shakespeare & Sons
BOOKS

23 🔒 Map p44, D2

Though its shelves groan with a formidable range of literature in English, French and German, this is more than just a bookshop (with Prague's best range of titles on East European history) – it's a congenial literary hang-out with knowledgeable staff, occasional author events, and a cool downstairs space for sitting and reading. (☎257 531 894; www.shakes.cz; U Lužického seminále 10; ⏰11am-9pm; 🚋12, 15, 20, 22)

Marionety Truhlář
ARTS & CRAFTS

24 🔒 Map p44, D2

This palace of puppetry stocks traditional marionettes from more than 40 workshops around the Czech Republic, as well as offering DIY puppet kits, courses on puppet-making, and the

Puppets from Marionety Truhlář

chance to order a custom-made marionette. (☎602 689 918; www.marionety.com; U Lužického seminále 5; ⏰10am-9pm; 🚋12, 15, 20, 22)

Artěl
GLASS, INTERIOR DESIGN

25 🔒 Map p44, D2

Traditional Bohemian glass-making meets modern design in this stylish shop founded by US designer Karen Feldman. In addition to hand-blown designer crystal, you can find a range of vintage and modern items of Czech design, from jewellery and ceramics to toys and stationery. (☎251 554 008; www.artelglass.com; U Lužickeho seminále 7; ⏰10am-7pm; 🚋12, 15, 20, 22)

Local Life
Beer & Culture in Smíchov

Standing in contrast to the fairy-tale historic sphere of castles and royal gardens, working-class Smíchov is a mainly industrial district on the Vltava's western bank. With its vibrant contemporary-art scene and unpretentious bars, the slightly gritty neighbourhood offers an authentic taste of Czech life, though its character is slowly changing with the construction of modern office complexes and an influx of new businesses.

Getting There

Ⓜ Line B to Anděl.

🚋 Lines 4, 5, 9, 10, 15, 16, 20 and 21 all pass through Smíchov, stopping at Anděl.

1 Jazz on the River

Jazz Dock (☎774 058 838; www.jazzdock.cz; Janáčkovo nábřeží 2, Smíchov; tickets 150-300Kč; ☉4pm-3am; 🛜; MAnděl, 🚊9, 12, 15, 20), Smíchov's riverside jazz venue, is a step up from the typical Prague club, with clean, modern decor and a romantic view out over the Vltava. It draws some of the best international acts. Go early or book to get a good table.

2 Avant-Garde Theatre at Švandovo Divadlo

The funky **Švandovo divadlo** (Švandovo Theatre in Smíchov; ☎box office 257 318 666; www.svandovodivadlo.cz; Štefánikova 57, Smíchov; tickets 150-300Kč; ☉box office 2-8pm Mon-Fri, plus 2hr before performances Sat & Sun; 🚊9, 12, 15, 20) stages avant-garde dramatic pieces, many with English subtitles, and acoustic music performances. It also hosts art exhibits and events.

3 Modern Art at Futura

The **Futura Gallery** (Centre for Contemporary Art Futura; ☎604 738 390; www.futuraproject.cz; Holečkova 49, Smíchov; admission by donation; ☉11am-6pm Wed-Sun; 🚊9, 12, 15, 20) is home to *Brown-nosers* (2003) by David Černý: stick your head inside the statue's backside to see a video of the former Czech president and the National Gallery's director feeding each other baby food.

4 Czech Food at Zlatý Klas

Cosy Pilsner Urquell restaurant **Zlatý Klas** (☎251 562 539; www.zlatyklas.cz; Plzeňská 9, Smíchov; mains 140-280Kč; ☉11am-11pm Sun-Thu, 11.30am-1am Fri & Sat; MAnděl) is beloved for its hearty, well-prepared Czech cuisine – try the killer 'Charles IV' baked pork ribs – plus ultrafresh *tankova* (tanked) beer.

5 Dancing at the 'Bulldog'

Popular pub **Hospoda U Buldoka** (At the Bulldog; ☎257 329 154; www.ubuldoka.cz; Preslova 1, Smíchov; ☉bar 11am-midnight Mon-Thu, 11am-1am Fri, noon-midnight Sat, noon-11pm Sun, club 8pm-4am Wed-Sat; 🛜; MAnděl) is a great place to drink – and a surprisingly good place to let your hair down, too. Don't expect sophisticated club ambience: this is a beer-fueled, dance-till-you-drop joint.

6 Beer at the Staropramen Brewery

To soak up some of Smíchov's down-to-earth charm – and feel the gentrification that's currently underway – pull up a barstool at **Na Verandách** (☎257 191 200; www.phnaverandach.cz; Nádražní 84, Smíchov; mains 150-280Kč; ☉11am-midnight Mon-Wed, to 1am Thu-Sat, to 11pm Sun; 🛜; MAnděl, 🚊4, 5, 12, 20), housed in the Staropramen Brewery (operating since 1871).

7 Cultural Events at 'Meet Factory'

For cutting-edge film screenings, concerts, theatrical performances and art installations, find out what's happening at David Černý's **Meet Factory** (☎251 551 796; www.meetfactory.cz; Ke Sklárně 15, Smíchov; admission free; ☉1-8pm, varies according to event; 🚊4, 5, 12, 20). Look for hanging red cars on the outside.

Explore

Jewish Museum & Josefov

Peaceful Josefov is the site of the former Jewish ghetto – the physical, cultural and spiritual home to the city's Jewish population for nearly 800 years. While many Jews left the quarter when it was renovated in the early 20th century (and tens of thousands were killed in the Holocaust), the surviving synagogues and cemetery make up the popular Jewish Museum.

The Sights in a Day

☀ Arrive at the **Jewish Museum** (p56) first thing in the morning and head for the **Old Jewish Cemetery** (p58) – the place is much more atmospheric when you're not with a huge crowd. Stop in at the **Maisel Synagogue** (p57) and the **Pinkas Synagogue** (p57), then take a well-deserved coffee break at **Bakeshop Praha** (p63) – and treat yourself to a chocolate croissant while you're at it. Properly caffeinated? Move on to a minitour of the beautiful **Spanish Synagogue** (p57).

☀ Stop for a late lunch – including a beer, of course – at classy corner pub **Kolkovna** (p63). You'll be near the **Franz Kafka Monument** (p62), which is fun for a quick look (and selfie). Spend the rest of the afternoon at either the **Museum of Decorative Arts** (p61) for design or the **Convent of St Agnes** (p62) for medieval and Gothic art.

☾ For dinner, there's **Lokál** (p62) for a classic Czech meal or **Kafka Snob Food** (p64) for something lighter. Afterwards, choose from a classical concert at the **Dvořák Hall** (p66) or opt for an edgier evening at the hollowed-out former theatre **Roxy** (p66). Before or after the show, stop in at **Tretter's New York Bar** (p64) for an expertly prepared martini.

◉ Top Sights

♥ Best of Prague

Getting There

Ⓜ **Metro** Line A to Staroměstská.

🚊 **Tram** Lines 2, 17, 18 to Staroměstská; lines 6, 8, 15, 26 to Dlouhá třída.

ANASTAZZO/SHUTTERSTOCK ©

Top Sights
Jewish Museum

Prague's Jewish Museum is among the city's most visited sights. It was established in 1906 to preserve artefacts from the quarter after it was razed and renovated in the late-19th and early-20th centuries. Exhibits are scattered among a handful of synagogues and focus on Jewish life and traditions. Highlights include the Pinkas Synagogue and its memorial to Czech and Moravian Jews killed in the Holocaust.

Map p60, B3

www.jewishmuseum.cz

Reservation Centre, Maiselova 15

ordinary ticket adult/child 300/200Kč, combined ticket incl Old-New Synagogue 480/320Kč

9am-6pm Sun-Fri Apr-Oct, to 4.30pm Nov-Mar

M Staroměstská

Spanish Synagogue

Klaus Synagogue & Ceremonial Hall

Both the baroque **Klaus Synagogue** (Klauzová synagóga; U starého hřbitova 1; incl in admission to Prague Jewish Museum; ☺9am-6pm Sun-Fri Apr-Oct, to 4.30pm Nov-Mar; 🚌17) and the nearby **Ceremonial Hall** (Obřadní síň; Old Jewish Cemetery; ☺9am-6pm Sun-Fri Apr-Oct, to 4.30pm Nov-Mar; 🚌17) contain exhibits on Jewish health and burial traditions and will be of most interest to historians or devout visitors.

Maisel Synagogue

Mordechai Maisel was mayor of the Jewish quarter under the liberal rule of Emperor Rudolf II during the 16th century. He was also the richest man in the city of Prague; in addition to various public works, he paid for this **synagogue** (Maiselova synagóga; Maiselova 10; incl in admission to Prague Jewish Museum; ☺9am-6pm Sun-Fri Apr-Oct, to 4.30pm Nov-Mar; Ⓜ Staroměstská) to be built for his private use. Today, it houses rotating exhibitions.

Pinkas Synagogue

Built in 1535, this **synagogue** (Pinkasova synagóga; Široká 3; incl in admission to Prague Jewish Museum; ☺9am-6pm Sun-Fri Apr-Oct, to 4.30pm Nov-Mar; Ⓜ Staroměstská) was used for worship until 1941; it's now a moving Holocaust memorial, its walls inscribed with the names, birth dates and dates of disappearance of 77,297 Czech Jews. Also here is a poignant exhibition of drawings made by children held at the Terezín concentration camp (north of Prague) during WWII.

Spanish Synagogue

Considered the most beautiful of the museum's synagogues, this 19th-century Moorish-style **building** (Španělská synagóga; Vězeňská 1; incl in admission to Prague Jewish Museum; ☺9am-6pm Sun-Fri Apr-Oct, to 4.30pm Nov-Mar; Ⓜ Staroměstská) boasts an ornate interior, an exhibition on recent Jewish history and a handy bookshop.

☑ Top Tips

▶ The museum is closed on Saturdays and Jewish holidays.

▶ Entry is by combined ticket only; it's not possible to visit the sites individually.

▶ Men must cover their heads. Yarmulkes (skullcaps) are provided at entrances.

▶ The Old-New Synagogue is not considered part of the museum and requires a separate admission ticket.

✕ Take a Break

Stop for some of the city's best gourmet coffee and pastries at nearby Bakeshop Praha (p63).

For a good pint of beer in the vicinity of the Spanish Synagogue, head to corner pub Kolkovna (p63).

Top Sights
Old Jewish Cemetery

City authorities once insisted that deceased Jews be interred only here – nowhere else – so by the time this cemetery stopped taking new burials in 1787 it was full to bursting. Today, it holds more than 12,000 tombstones – though as the Jewish Museum points out, many more than that are buried here. Be aware that conditions at this popular attraction sometimes feel almost as crowded for the living as for the dead.

◉ Map p60, A3

www.jewishmuseum.cz

Pinkas Synagogue, Široká 3

incl in admission to Prague Jewish Museum

🕑 9am-6pm Apr-Oct, to 4.30pm Nov-Mar

Ⓜ Staroměstská

Tombstones in the Old Jewish Cemetery

Rabbi Loew's Tomb

Sometimes called 'the Jewish hero of the Czechs', Rabbi Judah Loew ben Bezalel (1525–1609) was a respected scholar and the chief rabbi of Bohemia in the 16th century. Perhaps more importantly to Czech people, he's part of a legend surrounding the creation of the Golem, a creature he supposedly built from clay to protect the Jewish people living in Prague's ghetto.

Mordechai Maisel's Tomb

This tomb honours a philanthropist with some incredibly deep pockets. In addition to serving as a Jewish leader in the 16th century, Maisel was the city's wealthiest citizen. He paid for the construction of new buildings in the ghetto, had the roads paved, commissioned the Maisel Synagogue (p57) for his own private use and even lent money to Emperor Rudolf II.

David Gans' Tomb

A noted German historian and astronomer, Gans came to Prague in part to hear the lectures of Rabbi Loew. He's perhaps most famous for his association with Tycho Brahe, who asked Gans to translate the Alphonsine Tables from Hebrew to German.

Joseph Solomon Delmedigo's Tomb

Another impressive Jewish intellectual represented in the cemetery is Joseph Solomon Delmedigo, who was both a physician and a philosopher. He studied and worked all over Europe before finally settling in Prague in 1648 to write various scientific texts.

☑ Top Tips

▶ Entry to the cemetery is included in the general Jewish Museum admission ticket.

▶ Arrive early as the cemetery gets increasingly busy as the day goes on.

▶ Remember that you're in a cemetery – always be careful where you step.

✗ Take a Break

Stylish Mistral Cafe (p64) is a short walk from the cemetery and is great for coffee or food.

Also nearby is **U Rudolfina** (☏222 328 758; Křižovnická 10; ◷11am-10pm; Ⓜ Staroměstská), a down-to-earth local pub with some of the city's best Pilsner Urquell.

200 m
0.1 miles

Vltava River

Čech Bridge
(Čechův most)

Dvořákovo nábřeží

17 Haštalská

15 Rybná

Rybná

Prague Wheelchair Users Organisation

Benediktská

Kotva

Jakubská

5 ✕

Dlouhá

Masná

Malá Štupartská

Haštalské náměstí

Rámová

U obecního dvora

Masná

20

13

Convent of St Agnes
3

Týn Courtyard (Týnský dvůr)
Týnská

JOSEFOV

Kozí

Kozí

12
7
16
8 11
19
18
Dušní

Týnská ulička

V Kolkovně

Old Town Square (Staroměstské náměstí)

Bílkova

U Milosrdných

6

Vězeňská

Dušní

Franz Kafka Monument 4

Salvátorská

INTERCONTINENTAL Hotel

Elišky Krásnohorské

Pařížská

Pařížská

Jáchymova

PRAHA 1

Old-New Synagogue 1

Červená

Prague Jewish Museum

Široká

10

Maiselova

Kaprova

17.listopadu

Museum of Decorative Arts
2

Old Jewish Cemetery

Žatecka

Dvořákovo nábřeží

14

Jan Palach Square (náměstí Jana Palacha)

Staroměstská

Valentinská

9 ✕

Křižovnická

MAZIARZ/SHUTTERSTOCK ©

Old-New Synagogue

Sights

Old-New Synagogue SYNAGOGUE

 1 Map p60, B3

Completed around 1270, the Old-New Synagogue is Europe's oldest working synagogue and one of Prague's earliest Gothic buildings. You step down into it because it pre-dates the raising of Staré Město's street level in medieval times to guard against floods. Men must cover their heads (bring a hat or take one of the paper yarmulkes handed out at the entrance). Although the synagogue is one of the six Jewish monuments that make up the Prague Jewish Museum, entry is not included in the general admission ticket.

(Staronová synagóga; www.jewishmuseum. cz; Červená 2; adult/child 200/140Kč; ⊘9am-6pm Sun-Fri Apr-Oct, to 4.30pm Nov-Mar; 17)

Museum of Decorative Arts MUSEUM

2 Map p60, A3

This museum opened in 1900 as part of a European movement to encourage a return to the aesthetic values sacrificed to the Industrial Revolution. Its four halls are a feast for the eyes, full of 16th- to 19th-century artefacts such as furniture, tapestries, porcelain and a fabulous collection of glasswork. At the time of research it was closed due to extensive renovations taking

---

Understand
Golem City

- -

Tales of golems, or servants created from clay, date back to early Judaism. However, the most famous such mythical creature belonged to 16th-century Prague's Rabbi Loew, of the Old-New Synagogue. Loew is said to have used mud from the Vltava's banks to create a golem to protect the Prague ghetto. However, left alone one Sabbath, the creature ran amok and Rabbi Loew was forced to rush out of a service and remove the magic talisman that kept it moving. He then carried the lifeless body into the synagogue's attic, where some insist it remains. In 1915, Gustav Meyrink's novel *Der Golem* reprised the story and brought it into the European mainstream.

---

place; it was scheduled to reopen in 2017 with double the amount of space for its permanent exhibitions. (Umělecko-průmyslové muzeum; ☑251 093 111; www.upm.cz; 17.listopadu 2; adult/child 120/70Kč; ⏰10am-7pm Tue, to 6pm Wed-Sun; 2, 17, 18)

Convent of St Agnes   GALLERY

3 Map p60, D2

In the northeastern corner of Staré Město is the former Convent of St Agnes, Prague's oldest surviving Gothic building. The 1st-floor rooms hold the National Gallery's permanent collection of medieval and early Renaissance art (1200–1550) from Bohemia and Central Europe, a treasure house of glowing Gothic altar paintings and polychrome religious sculptures. (Klášter sv Anežky; ☑224 810 628; www.ngprague.cz; U Milosrdných 17; incl admission to all National Gallery venues, adult/child 300/150Kč; ⏰10am-6pm Tue-Sun; 🚊6, 8, 15, 26)

Franz Kafka Monument   MONUMENT

4 Map p60, C3

Commissioned by Prague's Franz Kafka Society in 2003, Jaroslav Róna's unusual sculpture of a mini-Kafka riding on the shoulders of a giant empty suit was based on the writer's story *Description of a Struggle*, in which the author explores a fantasy landscape from the shoulders of 'an acquaintance' (who may be another aspect of the author's personality). (cnr Vězeňská & Dušní; Ⓜ Staroměstská)

Eating

Lokál   CZECH €

5 Map p60, E3

Who'd have thought it possible? A classic Czech beer hall (albeit with slick modern styling); excellent *tankové pivo* (tanked Pilsner Urquell); a daily-changing menu of traditional

Bohemian dishes; and smiling, efficient, friendly service! Top restaurant chain Ambiente has turned its hand to Czech cuisine, and the result has been so successful that the place is always busy, mostly with locals. (☎222 316 265; http://lokal-dlouha.ambi.cz; Dlouhá 33; mains 115-235Kč; ☺11am-1am Mon-Sat, noon-midnight Sun; 🛜; 🚊6, 8, 15, 26)

Field
CZECH €€€

6 🍴 Map p60, C2

Prague's third Michelin-starred restaurant is its least formal and most fun. The decor is an amusing art-meets-agriculture blend of farmyard implements and minimalist chic, while the chef creates painterly presentations from the finest of local produce along with freshly foraged herbs and edible flowers. You'll have to book at least a couple of weeks in advance to have a chance of a table. (☎222 316 999; www.fieldrestaurant.cz; U Milosrdných 12; mains 590-620Kč, 6-course tasting menu 2800Kč; ☺11am-2.30pm & 6-10.30pm Mon-Fri, noon-3pm & 6-10.30pm Sat, noon-3pm & 6-10pm Sun; 🚊17)

Bakeshop Praha
BAKERY €

7 🍴 Map p60, D3

This fantastic bakery sells some of the best bread in the city, along with pastries, cakes and takeaway sandwiches, wraps, salads and quiche. Very busy at lunchtime. (☎222 316 823; www.bakeshop.cz; Kozí 1; sandwiches 75-200Kč; ☺7am-9pm; Ⓜ Staroměstská)

Convent of St Agnes

Kolkovna
CZECH €€

8 🍴 Map p60, C3

Owned and operated by the Pilsner Urquell Brewery, Kolkovna is a stylish, modern take on the traditional Prague pub, with decor by top Czech designers, and posh (but hearty) versions of classic Czech dishes such as goulash, roast duck and Moravian sparrow, as well as the Czech favourite, roast pork knuckle. All washed down with exquisite Urquell beer, of course. (☎224 819 701; www.vkolkovne.cz; V Kolkovně 8; mains 120-390Kč; ☺11am-midnight; 🛜; Ⓜ Staroměstská)

Mistral Café

9 🍴 Map p60, A4   BISTRO €

Is this the coolest bistro in the Old Town? Pale stone, bleached birchwood and potted shrubs make for a clean, crisp, modern look, and the clientele of local students and office workers clearly appreciate the competitively priced, well-prepared food. Fish and chips in crumpled brown paper with lemon and black-pepper mayo – yum! (📞222 317 737; www.mistralcafe.cz; Valentinská 11; mains 130-250Kč; ⏱10am-11pm; 🛜♿; Ⓜ Staroměstská)

Kafka Snob Food

10 🍴 Map p60, B4   ITALIAN €€

A favourite hang-out for fashion-conscious employees of the Old Town's many designer boutiques, this smoky bistro models a self-consciously hip look that combines turquoise-painted panelling and tan leather banquettes with brushed steel ducting and painted brick. The menu offers authentically Italian pasta and risotto dishes, plus great cakes and coffee. And no, we don't know what the name means either. (📞725 915 505; www.facebook.com/kafkasnobfood; Široká 12; mains 150-300Kč; ⏱8am-10pm; 🛜✍; Ⓜ Staroměstská)

Drinking

Tretter's New York Bar

11 🍷 Map p60, C3   BAR

This sultry 1930s Manhattan-style cocktail bar harks back to gentler times when people went out for nightcaps – and when the drinks were stiff and properly made. Regularly cited as one of the city's top bars, Tretter's brings in the beautiful people and has prices to match. Book your table in advance. (📞224 811 165; www.tretters.cz; V Kolkovně 3; ⏱7pm-2am; Ⓜ Staroměstská)

Kozička

12 🍷 Map p60, D3   BAR

The 'Little Goat' is a buzzing, red-brick basement bar decorated with cute steel goat sculptures, serving Krušovice on tap at 55Kč for 0.5L (though watch out – the bartenders will occasionally sling you a 1L *tuplák* if they think you're a tourist). It fills up later in the evening with a mostly Czech crowd, and makes a civilised setting for a late-night session. (📞224 818 308; www.kozicka.cz; Kozí 1; ⏱4pm-4am Mon-Thu, 5pm-5.30am Fri, 6pm-5.30am Sat, 7pm-3am Sun; 🛜; Ⓜ Staroměstská)

Prague Beer Museum

13 🍷 Map p60, E3   PUB

Although the name seems aimed at the tourist market, this lively and always-heaving pub pulls in some locals too, especially at lunchtime. There are no fewer than 30 Czech-produced craft beers on tap (plus a beer menu with tasting notes to guide you). Try a sample board – a wooden platter with five 0.15L glasses containing five beers of your choice. (📞732 330 912; www.praguebeermuseum.com; Dlouhá 46; ⏱noon-3am; 🛜; 🚊6, 8, 15, 26)

Understand

Jewish Prague

Jews have been part of Prague for as long as it has existed, though their status has ebbed and flowed. For centuries, Jews were restricted to living in a small corner of the Old Town (today's Josefov). Some periods brought terror and pogroms, while others – the early 17th century – brought prosperity. In the 19th century, Jews were allowed to live outside their ghetto, but a century later most were murdered by the occupying Nazis.

Early Oppression

Jews began living in Prague in the 10th century, and by the 11th century the city was one of Europe's most important Jewish centres. The Crusades marked the start of the Jews' plight as the city's oldest synagogue was burned to the ground. By the end of the 12th century, they lost many rights; soon they were forced into a walled ghetto that was locked at night. For years, Jews remained third-class citizens while emperors and the nobility argued over who should be in charge of Jewish affairs.

The Golden Age

The mid-16th-to-early-17th century is considered the golden age of Jewish history. Emperor Rudolf II (r 1576–1612) worked closely with Mayor Mordechai Maisel (1528–1601), at the time the wealthiest man in Prague. The community was led in spirit by noted mystic and Talmudic scholar Rabbi Loew (1525–1609).

Emancipation came in the 18th century under Habsburg Emperor Josef II. In 1848, Jews won the right of abode, meaning they could live where they wanted. The ghetto's walls were torn down and the Jewish quarter was renamed Josefov (to honour Josef II). As wealthy Jews moved out, the area slid into squalor. At the end of the 19th century, the area was levelled and rebuilt in art nouveau splendour.

Destruction & Preservation

The Jewish community was largely destroyed by the Nazis in WWII, and only a few thousand Jews remain. One historic irony is that many of the Jewish Museum's holdings come from *shtetls* (Jewish villages) liquidated by the Nazis. Hitler had the artefacts brought here, chillingly, to build a 'museum of an extinct race'.

POPOVA VALERIYA/SHUTTERSTOCK ©

Dvořák Hall

Roxy

LIVE MUSIC

15 ⭐ Map p60, E2

Set in the ramshackle shell of an art-deco cinema, the legendary Roxy has nurtured the more independent and innovative end of Prague's club spectrum since 1987 – this is the place to see the Czech Republic's top DJs. On the 1st floor is NoD, an 'experimental space' that stages drama, dance, performance art, cinema and live music. Best nightspot in Staré Město. (☎224 826 296; www.roxy.cz; Dlouhá 33; tickets 150-700Kč; ⏰7pm-5am; 🚊6, 8, 15, 26)

Shopping

TEG1

FASHION & ACCESSORIES

16 🔒 Map p60, C3

TEG (Timoure et Group) is the design team created by Alexandra Pavalová and Ivana Šafránková, two of Prague's most respected fashion designers. This boutique showcases their quarterly collections, which feature a sharp, imaginative look that adds zest and sophistication to everyday, wearable clothes. There's a second **branch** (☎224 240 737; Martinská 4; 🅼Národní Třída) near Národní třída. (☎222 327 358; www.timoure.cz; V Kolkovně 6; ⏰10am-7pm Mon-Fri, 11am-5pm Sat; 🅼Staroměstská)

Entertainment

Dvořák Hall

CONCERT VENUE

14 ⭐ Map p60, A3

The Dvořák Hall in the neo-Renaissance **Rudolfinum** (☎227 059 270; Alšovo nábřeží 12; 🚊2, 17, 18) is home to the world-renowned Czech Philharmonic Orchestra (Česká filharmonie). Sit back and be impressed by some of the best classical musicians in Prague. (Dvořákova síň; ☎227 059 227; www.ceskafilharmonie.cz; náměstí Jana Palacha 1, Rudolfinum; tickets 120-900Kč; ⏰box office 10am-12.30pm & 1.30-6pm Mon-Fri; 🅼Staroměstská)

Gurmet Pasáž Dlouhá

FOOD & DRINKS

17 Map p60, E2

Prague's foodie scene attains its apotheosis in this upmarket arcade dedicated to fine food. As well as eateries such as Nase Maso and Banh Mi Makers, you'll find shops selling fine wines, artisanal cheeses, handmade chocolate and imported seafood. (Gourmet Arcade; www.gurmetpasazdlouha. eu; Dlouhá 39; ◷9am-10pm)

Klara Nademlýnská

FASHION & ACCESSORIES

18 Map p60, C4

Klara Nademlýnská is one of the Czech Republic's top fashion designers, having trained in Prague and worked for almost a decade in Paris. Her clothes are characterised by clean lines, simple styling and quality materials, making for a very wearable range that covers the spectrum from swimwear to evening wear via jeans, blouses and suits. (☑224 818 769; www. klaranademlynska.cz; Dlouhá 3; ◷10am-7pm Mon-Fri, to 6pm Sat; Ⓜ Staroměstská)

Bohème

FASHION & ACCESSORIES

19 Map p60, C3

This boutique showcases the designs of Hana Stocklassa and her associates, with collections of knitwear, leather and suede clothes for women. There's a range of jewellery to choose from as well. (☑224 813 840; www.boheme.cz;

Ⓠ Local Life

Home of Fashion Boutiques

Josefov is home to the nascent Czech fashion scene, particularly small, independent boutiques that highlight the best of local and international design. For the latter, check out **Dušní 3** (☑234 095 870; www.dusni3.cz; Dušní 3; ◷10am-7pm Mon-Sat; Ⓜ Staroměstská), a self-styled alternative to the megabrand stores on nearby Pařížská. You'll find a range of ready-to-wear fashion and accessories from top designers, including Tara Jarmon, Ilaria Nistri and Vivienne Westwood. They've got an excellent line of shoes and sunglasses as well.

Dušní 8; ◷11am-7pm Mon-Fri, to 5pm Sat; Ⓜ Staroměstská)

Granát Turnov

JEWELLERY

20 Map p60, D3

Part of the country's biggest jewellery chain, Granát Turnov specialises in Bohemian garnet, and has a huge range of gold and silver rings, brooches, cufflinks and necklaces featuring these small, dark blood-red stones. There's also pearl and diamond jewellery, and less expensive pieces set with the dark green semiprecious stone known in Czech as *vltavín* (moldavite). (☑222 315 612; www.granat.eu; Dlouhá 28-30; ◷10am-6pm Mon-Fri, to 1pm Sat; Ⓜ Náměstí Republiky)

Explore

Old Town Square & Staré Město

Staré Město (Old Town), with its evocative medieval square, maze of alleyways, and quirky sights like the Astronomical Clock, is the beating heart of the historic centre. Its origins date back to the 10th century, when a marketplace emerged on the Vltava's eastern bank. A thousand years later, it's as alive as ever, and surprisingly little changed by time.

The Sights in a Day

☀ For the quietest experience and most magical views of **Charles Bridge** (p72), start your morning as early as possible. Start on the Malá Strana side and cross the bridge towards the Old Town. Be sure to climb the **Old Town Bridge Tower** (p73). Then make a beeline for the **Astronomical Clock** (p71) to catch the famous hourly chiming before the tourist crowds start to multiply.

☀ Afterwards, take the lift up the **Old Town Hall Tower** (p71) for views over Old Town Sq and the historic centre. Have a leisurely lunch at **Kalina** (p77), sampling gourmet versions of Czech dishes from the tasting menu. Then, wander the quaint cobblestone backstreets around Betlémské náměstí, stopping in to see Jan Hus' old stomping ground at **Bethlehem Chapel** (p76).

☾ As night falls, head back to Old Town Sq to view the beautifully illuminated **Church of St Nicholas** (p71) and **Church of Our Lady Before Týn** (p71). Have dinner on the terrace of **U Prince** (p77) or take a glass of Moravian wine in a glamorous setting at the **Municipal House's cafe** (p79). Catch some live jazz at **AghaRTA Jazz Centrum** (p80) to finish off the day.

Top Sights

Old Town Square (p70) & Astronomical Clock (p71)

Charles Bridge (p72)

♥ Best of Prague

Bars & Pubs

Hemingway Bar (p80)

Čili Bar (p80)

U Tří růží (p78)

Food

V Zátiší (p78)

Kalina (p77)

Art

Hanging Out (Viselec) (p77)

Municipal House (p77)

Museums

Charles Bridge Museum (p73)

Kinský Palace (p76)

Getting There

Ⓜ **Metro** Take line A to Staroměstská (the closest stop to Old Town Square) or line A or B to Můstek.

🚊 **Tram** Lines 2, 17 and 18 run to Staroměstská; lines 6, 8, 15 and 26 stop at Dlouhá třída.

Top Sights
Old Town Square & Astronomical Clock

Laid with cobblestones and surrounded by spectacular baroque churches, soaring spires, candy-coloured buildings and a rococo palace, Old Town Sq is an architectural smorgasbord and a photographer's delight. While the Astronomical Clock – a mechanical marvel that still chimes on the hour – is more than 600 years old, many of the structures in Old Town Sq are even older: settlers started moving here across the river from Prague Castle as far back as the 10th century.

Staroměstské náměstí

⊙ Map p74, C2

Ⓜ Staroměstská

Astronomical Clock

Astronomical Clock

Built in 1490 by a master clockmaker named Hanuš, the **Astronomical Clock** (⏰chimes on the hour 9am-9pm; Ⓜ Staroměstská) was a scientific feat in its day – even after various renovations, it remains a paradigm of antique technology. On the hour, crowds gather below for its quaint visual display.

Old Town Hall Clock Tower

Old Town Hall, dating from 1338, has more to offer than its clock. Climb (or take the lift) up the **clock tower** (Věž radnice; ☎236 002 629; www.staromestskaradnicepraha.cz; Staroměstské náměstí 1; adult/child 130/80Kč, incl Old Town Hall tour 180Kč; ⏰11am-10pm Mon, 9am-10pm Tue-Sun; Ⓜ Staroměstská) for privileged views over Old Town Sq and the historic city centre.

Jan Hus Statue

Sitting near the centre of the square, Ladislav Šaloun's brooding art nouveau statue of Jan Hus was unveiled on 6 July 1915, the 500th anniversary of Hus' death at the stake.

Church of Our Lady Before Týn

Straight out of a 15th-century fairy tale, the spiky, spooky Gothic spires of **Church of Our Lady Before Týn** (Kostel Panny Marie před Týnem; www.tyn.cz; Staroměstské náměstí; suggested donation 25Kč; ⏰10am-1pm & 3-5pm Tue-Sat, 10am-noon Sun Mar-Dec; Ⓜ Staroměstská), aka Týn Church, are an unmistakable Old Town landmark. It also houses the tomb of Tycho Brahe.

Church of St Nicholas

This pretty baroque **monastery** (Kostel sv Mikuláše; www.svmikulas.cz; Staroměstské náměstí; admission free; ⏰10am-4pm Mon-Sat, noon-4pm Sun; Ⓜ Staroměstská) is relatively new: finished in 1735, it replaced a Gothic church built here in the late 13th century. After several incarnations it now serves as a Czechoslovak Hussite church and a classical concert venue.

☑ Top Tips

▶ For the best views of the Astronomical Clock, come to the chiming at 9am or 10am. Arrive a few minutes before the hour.

▶ Look for lively food and craft stalls in Old Town Sq around major holidays like Christmas and Easter.

▶ Climb (or take the lift) up the clock tower for spectacular views over Old Town Sq. Again, earlier is better.

▶ The most romantic time to visit the square is after dark, when the medieval buildings are beautifully illuminated.

✗ Take a Break

Have a gourmet lunch at Kalina (p77), where fresh Czech produce is given a serious gastronomic twist

At night, you're spoiled for choice. Čili Bar (p80) is a perfect romantic hideway. Hemingway Bar (p80) has the city's best cocktails, but reserve in advance.

Top Sights
Charles Bridge

You know a historic landmark is something special when even the crush of tourist traffic hardly takes away from its magnificence. So it is with Charles Bridge, Prague's signature monument. Commissioned in 1357, the massive, 520m-long stone bridge was the only link across the Vltava River between Prague Castle and the Old Town until 1741. It's particularly awe-inspiring at dawn, when the silhouettes of saintly statues along both sides seem to guide you towards the towering hilltop fortress.

Karlův most

👁 Map p74, A2

🕙 24hr

🚊 2, 17, 18 to Karlovy lázně, 12, 15, 20, 22 to Malostranské náměstí

Charles Bridge

View from the Old Town Bridge Tower

Perched at the eastern end of Charles Bridge, the elegant late-14th-century **Old Town Bridge Tower** (Staroměstská mostecká věž; ☎224 220 569; http://en.muzeumprahy.cz/prague-towers; Charles Bridge; adult/child 90/65Kč; ☉10am-10pm Apr-Sep, to 8pm Mar & Oct, to 6pm Nov-Feb; ☐17, 18) was built not only as a fortification but also as a triumphal arch marking the entrance to the Old Town. Head upstairs for the dramatic view down over the crowded bridge.

Saintly Statues

The first monument erected on the bridge was the crucifix near the eastern end, in 1657. The first statue – the Jesuits' 1683 tribute to St John of Nepomuk – inspired other Catholic orders, and over the next 30 years a score more went up. Today most are copies, but a few of the originals can be seen at the **Brick Gate & Casements** at the Vyšehrad Citadel.

Rubbing St John of Nepomuk

The most famous statue is that of **St John of Nepomuk**, on the northern side of the bridge about halfway across. According to legend, Wenceslas IV had him thrown off the bridge in 1393 for refusing to divulge the queen's confessions (he was her priest). Tradition says, if you rub the bronze plaque, you will one day return to Prague.

Charles Bridge Museum

Examine the history of the Vltava's most famous crossing at the **Charles Bridge Museum** (Muzeum Karlova Mostu; ☎776 776 779; www.charlesbridgemuseum.com; Křížovnické náměstí 3; adult/concession 170/70Kč; ☉10am-6pm; ☐2, 17, 18), located near the bridge's Old Town entrance. When you learn about the bridge's tumultuous 650-year history, including at least two perilous encounters with floods, you'll be surprised it's still standing.

☑ Top Tips

▶ Visit the bridge early in the day to beat the crowds.

▶ Keep your valuables close at hand: pickpockets lurk here, especially in summer.

▶ Plan to cross the bridge at least twice – once towards the castle and once away from it.

▶ Sunrise is the ideal time for photos. In winter if it starts snowing, head for the bridge to capture some unforgettable images.

✗ Take a Break

Not far from the entrance to the Old Town side of the bridge, the student cafe Cafe Kampus (p80) is a great place to relax over a coffee or beer.

Splurge on a gourmet meal paired with Czech wine at Bellevue (p78) or V zátiší (p78); both are close to the Old Town side of the bridge.

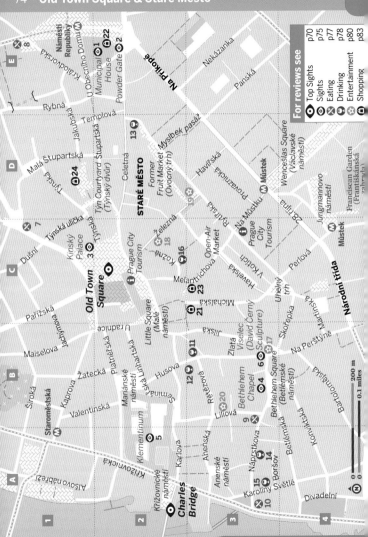

VARNAKOV/SHUTTERSTOCK ©

Municipal House

Sights

Municipal House   HISTORIC BUILDING

1  Map p74, E2

Restored in the 1990s after decades of neglect, Prague's most exuberantly art-nouveau building is a labour of love, every detail of its design and decoration carefully considered, every painting and sculpture loaded with symbolism. The **restaurant** (222 002 770; www.francouzskarestaurace.cz; Municipal House; mains 695Kč; noon-11pm) and **cafe** (p79) here are like walk-in museums of art-nouveau design, while upstairs there are half a dozen sumptuously decorated halls that you can visit by guided tour. (Obecní dům;

222 002 101; www.obecnidum.cz; náměstí Republiky 5; guided tour adult/concession/ child under 10yr 290/240Kč/free; public areas 7.30am-11pm, information centre 10am-8pm; M Náměstí Republiky, 6, 8, 15, 26)

Powder Gate   TOWER

2  Map p74, E2

Construction of the 65m-tall Powder Gate was begun in 1475 on the site of one of Staré Město's 13 original city gates. The exterior is a froth of Gothic decoration, while the interior houses little more than a few information panels about the tower's construction – the main attraction is the view from the top. (Prašná brána; http://en.muzeumprahy.cz/prague-towers;

Na příkopě; adult/child 90/65Kč; ⏱10am-10pm Apr-Sep, to 8pm Oct & Mar, to 6pm Nov-Feb; Ⓜ Náměstí Republiky)

Kinský Palace　　　GALLERY

3 ⊙ Map p74, C1

The late-baroque Kinský Palace sports Prague's finest rococo facade, completed in 1765 by the redoubtable Kilian Dientzenhofer. Today the palace is home to a branch of the National Gallery, housing its collection of ancient and oriental art, ranging from ancient Egyptian tomb treasures and Greek Apulian pottery (4th century BC) to Chinese and Japanese decorative art and calligraphy. (Palác Kinských; ☏ 224 810 758; www.ngprague.cz; Staroměstské náměstí 12; incl admission to all National Gal-lery venues; adult/child 300/150Kč; ⏱10am-6pm Tue-Sun; Ⓟ; Ⓜ Staroměstská)

Bethlehem Chapel　　　CHURCH

4 ⊙ Map p74, B3

The Bethlehem Chapel is a national cultural monument, being the birthplace of the Hussite cause. Jan Hus preached here from 1402 to 1412, marking the emergence of the Reform movement from the sanctuary of the Karolinum (where he was rector). Every year on the night of 5 July, the eve of Hus's burning at the stake in 1415, a memorial is held here with speeches and bell-ringing. (Betlémská kaple; ☏ 224 248 595; www.bethlehem-chapel.eu; Betlémské náměstí 3; adult/child 60/30Kč; ⏱10am-6pm; 🚊2, 9, 18, 22)

Understand
The Astronomical Clock's Spectacle

Every hour on the hour, crowds gather beneath the Old Town Hall Tower to watch the Astronomical Clock in action. It's an amusing – if slightly underwhelming – performance that takes just under a minute to finish. Most people simply stand and gawk, but it's worth understanding a bit of the clock's historic (and highly photogenic) symbolism.

The four figures beside the clock represent the deepest civic anxieties of 15th-century Praguers: Vanity (with a mirror), Greed (with his telltale money bag), Death (the skeleton) and Pagan Invasion (represented by a Turk). The four figures below these are the Chronicler, Angel, Astronomer and Philosopher.

On the hour, Death rings a bell and inverts his hourglass, and the Twelve Apostles parade past the windows above the clock, nodding to the crowd. On the left side are Paul (with a sword and a book), Thomas (lance), Jude (book), Simon (saw), Bartholomew (book) and Barnabas (parchment); on the right side are Peter (with a key), Matthew (axe), John (snake), Andrew (cross), Philip (cross) and James (mallet). At the end, a cock crows and the hour is rung.

Klementinum
HISTORIC BUILDING

5 Map p74, A2

The Klementinum is a vast complex of beautiful baroque and rococo halls, now mostly occupied by the Czech National Library. Most of the buildings are closed to the public, but you can walk freely through the courtyards, or take a 50-minute guided tour of the baroque Library Hall, the Meridian Hall, the Astronomical Tower and (if no events are taking place) the Chapel of Mirrors. (📞606 100 293; www.klementinum.com; entrances on Křížovnická, Karlova & Mariánské náměstí; guided tour adult/child 220/140Kč; 🕑10am-5pm Apr-Oct, to 4pm Nov, Dec & Mar; Ⓜ Staroměstská, 🚊2, 17, 18)

Viselec (David Černý Sculpture)
SCULPTURE

6 Map p74, B3

Here's some more inspired madness from artist David Černý: look up as you walk along Husova street and you'll see a bearded, bespectacled chap not unlike Sigmund Freud casually dangling by one hand from a pole way above the ground. (Hanging Out; www.davidcerny.cz; Husova; 🚊2, 9, 18, 22)

Eating

Kalina
FRENCH €€€

7 Map p74, C1

Setting a trend for taking the best of fresh Czech produce and giving it the French gourmet treatment, this smart

 Top Tip

Views Of Old Town Square

The food might not be brilliant atop **U Prince** (📞737 261 842; www.hoteluprince.com; Staroměstské náměstí 29; mains 230-550Kč; 🕑11am-11pm; Ⓜ Můstek), but the bird's-eye view of Old Town Sq is unforgettable. Find its rooftop terrace by taking the lift at the back of the entrance hall to the top and climbing the stairs from there.

but unfailingly friendly little restaurant offers dishes such as Prague snails with beef marrow and parsley purée, and roast sweetbreads with glazed salsify and black truffles. Weekday lunch specials are good value at between 150Kč and 300Kč. (📞222 317 715; www.kalinarestaurant.cz; Dlouhá 12; mains 500-900Kč; 🕑noon-3pm & 6-11.30pm; 🛜; 🚊6, 8, 15, 26)

Ambiente Pizza Nuova
ITALIAN €€

8 Map p74, E1

This cool 1st-floor space filled with big tables and banquettes with picture windows overlooking náměstí Republiky showcases a good idea from the Ambiente team: for a fixed price (298Kč per person before 6pm, 385Kč after) you get an all-you-can-eat pasta and pizza deal. (Adding an antipasti buffet to the pizza-pasta deal costs 485/578Kč.) Wine by the glass costs from 88Kč to 198Kč. (📞221 803 308; http://pizzanuova.ambi.cz; Revoluční 1; mains 200-500Kč; 🕑11.30am-11.30pm; 🛜; Ⓜ Náměstí Republiky)

V Zátiší
CZECH, INDIAN €€€

9 Map p74, B3

'Still Life' is one of Prague's top restaurants, famed for the quality of its cuisine. The decor is bold and modern, with quirky glassware, boldly patterned wallpapers and cappuccino-coloured crushed-velvet chairs. The menu ranges from high-end

 Local Life

Going Meatless in Staré Město

Prague's oldest quarter is home to several good vegetarian and vegan spots. Our favourites:

Country Life (☏224 213 366; www.countrylife.cz; Melantrichova 15; mains 90-180Kč; ⏱10.30am-7.30pm Mon-Thu, to 3.30pm Fri, noon-6pm Sun; 🛜🍴; Ⓜ Můstek) All-vegan cafeteria offering inexpensive salads, vegetarian goulash, sunflower-seed burgers and soy drinks.

Lehká Hlava (☏222 220 665; www.lehkahlava.cz; Boršov 2; mains 200-240Kč; ⏱11.30am-11.30pm Mon-Fri, noon-11.30pm Sat & Sun; 🍴🚼; 🚃2, 17, 18) Down a narrow cul-de-sac, this simple, student-friendly spot exists in a little world of its own.

Maitrea (☏221 711 631; www.restaurace-maitrea.cz; Týnská ulička 6; mains 200-240Kč; weekday lunch 135Kč; ⏱11.30am-11.30pm Mon-Fri, noon-11.30pm Sat & Sun; 🍴🚼; Ⓜ Staroměstská) Beautifully designed space with inventive vegetarian dishes.

Indian cuisine to gourmet versions of traditional Czech dishes – the South Bohemian duck with white cabbage and herb dumplings is superb. (☏222 221 155; www.vzatisi.cz; Liliová 1; 2-/3-course meal 990/1190Kč; ⏱noon-3pm & 5.30-11pm; 🛜; 🚃2, 17, 18)

Bellevue
INTERNATIONAL €€€

10 Map p74, A3

Book a table on the terrace and come to enjoy the fabulous views of the river and castle while tucking into gourmet cuisine. Bellevue offers a Eurasian choice of dishes from roasted veal loin in black-truffle crust to New Zealand lamb chops marinated in lemon thyme. Best value is the three-course set menu. (☏224 221 443; www.bellevuerestaurant.cz; Smetanovo nábř 18; mains 845Kč, 3-course set menu 1490Kč; ⏱11am-11pm; 🍴; 🚃2, 17, 18)

Drinking

U Tří Růží
BREWERY

11 Map p74, B3

In the 19th century there were more than 20 breweries in Prague's Old Town, but by 1989 there was only one left (U Medvidku). The Three Roses brewpub, on the site of one of those early breweries, helps revive the tradition, offering six beers on tap, including a tasty *světlý ležák* (pale lager; 56Kč per 0.4L), good food and convivial surroundings. (☏601 588 281; www.u3r.cz; Husova 10; ⏱11am-11pm Sun-Thu, to midnight Fri & Sat; 🚃2, 17, 18)

OSCITY/SHUTTERSTOCK ©

Grand Cafe Orient

U Zlatého Tygra

PUB

12   Map p74, B3

Novelist Bohumil Hrabal's favourite hostelry, the 'Golden Tiger' is one of the few Old Town drinking holes that has hung on to its soul – and its reasonable prices (45Kč per 0.45L of Pilsner Urquell), considering its location close to Old Town Square. A thick fug of cigarette smoke keeps many tourists away. (222 221 111; www.uzlatehotygra.cz; Husova 17; 3-11pm; Staroměstská)

Kavárna Obecní Dům

CAFE

The spectacular cafe in Prague's opulent **Municipal House** (see 1   Map p74, E2) offers the opportunity to sip your cappuccino amid an orgy of art-nouveau splendour. (222 002 763; www.kavarnaod.cz; náměstí Republiky 5, Municipal House; 7.30am-11pm; Náměstí Republiky)

Grand Cafe Orient

CAFE

13   Map p74, D2

Prague's only cubist cafe, the Orient was designed by Josef Gočár in 1912 and flaunts its cubist styling down to the smallest detail, including the lampshades and coat hooks. It was restored and reopened in 2005, having been closed since 1920. Decent coffee and inexpensive cocktails, but occasionally surly service. (224 224 240; www.grandcafeorient.cz; Ovocný trh 19;

9am-10pm Mon-Fri, 10am-10pm Sat & Sun; Náměstí Republiky)

Café Kampus
CAFE

14 Map p74, A3

This cool cafe doubles as an art gallery and occasional music venue, and is hugely popular with students from nearby Charles University. There are Czech newspapers and books to leaf through, chilled tunes on the sound system, and a menu of gourmet teas and coffees to choose from. (📞 775 755 143; www.cafekampus.cz; Náprstkova 10; ⏰ 10am-1am Mon-Fri, noon-1am Sat, noon-11pm Sun; 🛜; 🚋 2, 17, 18)

Hemingway Bar
COCKTAIL BAR

15 Map p74, A3

The Hemingway is a snug and sophisticated hideaway with dark leather benches, a library-like back room, flickering candlelight, and polite and professional bartenders. There's a huge range of quality spirits (especially rum), first-class cocktails, champagne and cigars. (📞 773 974 764; www.hemingwaybar.eu; Karolíny Světlé 26; ⏰ 5pm-1am Mon-Thu, to 2am Fri, 7pm-2am Sat, 7pm-1am Sun; 🛜; 🚋 2, 17, 18)

Čili Bar
COCKTAIL BAR

16 Map p74, C2

This tiny cocktail bar could not be further removed in atmosphere from your typical Old Town drinking place. Cramped and smoky – there are Cuban cigars for sale – with battered leather armchairs competing for space with a handful of tables, it's friendly, relaxed and lively. Try the speciality of the house – rum mixed with finely chopped red chillis (minimum three shots). (📞 724 379 117; www.cilibar.cz; Kožná 8; ⏰ 6pm-2am; 🛜; Můstek)

Entertainment

Jazz Republic
LIVE MUSIC

17 Map p74, B3

Despite the name, this relaxed club stages all kinds of live music, including rock, blues, reggae and fusion as well as jazz. Bands are mostly local, and the music is not overpowering – you can easily hold a conversation – which means it won't please the purists (sssshh!). (📞 221 183 552; www.jazzrepublic.cz; Jilská 1a; admission free; ⏰ 8pm-late, music 9.15pm-midnight; Národní Třída)

AghaRTA Jazz Centrum
JAZZ

18 Map p74, C2

AghaRTA has been staging top-notch modern jazz, blues, funk and fusion since 1991, but moved into this central Old Town venue only in 2004. A typical jazz cellar with red-brick vaults, the centre also has a music shop (open 7pm to midnight) which sells CDs, T-shirts and coffee mugs. As well as hosting local musicians, AghaRTA occasionally stages gigs by leading international artists. (📞 222 211 275; www.

Understand

Literary Prague

Prague has a well-deserved reputation as a literary heavyweight. The names Franz Kafka and Milan Kundera will be familiar to any serious reader, but Prague's writing roots run deeper – it's no accident the country's first postcommunist president, Václav Havel, was a playwright. In addition to its Czech writers, the city was also once a hotbed of German literature.

Czech Literary Lights

Besides the clever Kundera (b 1929), a staple on undergrad reading lists, Prague was home to humourist Bohumil Hrabal (1914–97), whose many books are widely translated into English. The film based on his novel *Closely Watched Trains* won the Oscar for Best Foreign Film in 1968. Another near-household name is Jaroslav Hašek (1883–1923), whose book *The Good Soldier Švejk* is a stroke of comic genius that recalls something of *Catch-22*. Czech poet Jaroslav Seifert won the Nobel Prize for poetry in 1984.

The German Connection

In the 19th and early 20th centuries, Prague was a centre of German literature. Kafka (1883–1924), a German-speaking Jewish writer, re-mains the gold standard: his books *The Trial* and *The Castle*, among many others, are modern classics. But Prague was also home to Kafka's friend and publisher Max Brod (1883–1924), as well as noted writers Egon Erwin Kisch (1885–1948) and Franz Werfel (1890–1945). One of the most beloved poets in the German language, Rainer Maria Rilke (1875–1926), was born and studied in Prague.

New Voices

There's no shortage of new Czech literary talent: Jáchym Topol (b 1962), Petra Hůlová (b 1979), Michal Viewegh (b 1962), Michal Ajvaz (b 1949), Emil Hakl (b 1958) and Miloš Urban (b 1967) are taking their places among the country's leading authors. They are pushing out old-guard figures such as Kundera, now seen as chroniclers of a very different, postcommunist age. Until recently, few books from these younger novel-ists had been translated into English. That's changing slowly, however, as publishers appear more willing to take a chance on marketing them to English-speaking audiences.

agharta.cz; Železná 16; cover 250Kč; ⊘7pm-1am, music 9pm-midnight; Ⓜ Můstek)

Smetana Hall

CLASSICAL MUSIC

The Smetana Hall, centrepiece of the stunning **Municipal House** (see 1 ◉ Map p74, E2), is the city's largest concert hall, with seating for 1200 beneath an art-nouveau glass dome. The stage is framed by sculptures representing the Vyšehrad legend (to the right) and Slavonic dances (to the left). This is the home venue of the Prague Symphony Orchestra (Symfonický orchestr hlavního města Prahy; www.fok.cz), and also stages performances of folk dance and music. (Smetanova síň; ☎222 002 101; www.obecnidum.cz; náměstí Republiky 5, Municipal House; tickets 400–900Kč; ⊘box office 10am-6pm; Ⓜ Náměstí Republiky)

Estates Theatre

OPERA, BALLET

19 ⭐ Map p74, D3

The Estates is the oldest theatre in Prague, famed as the place where Mozart conducted the premiere of *Don Giovanni* on 29 October 1787. This, and other Mozart operas, are regularly performed here, along with a range of classic opera, ballet and drama productions. (Stavovské divadlo; ☎224 902 322; www.narodni-divadlo.cz; Ovocný trh 1; tickets 100–990Kč; ⊘box office 10am-6pm; Ⓜ Můstek)

Blues Sklep

JAZZ

20 ⭐ Map p74, B3

One of the city's newer jazz clubs, the Blues Sklep (*sklep* means 'cellar') is a typical Old Town basement with dark, Gothic-vaulted rooms that provide an atmospheric setting for regular

---

Understand
The Trials of Tycho Brahe

It's probably more than fair to describe Tycho Brahe, who's buried in the Church of Our Lady Before Týn (p71), as something of a character. This Danish father of modern astronomy catalogued thousands of stars, made stunningly accurate observations in an era before telescopes, and helped his assistant Johannes Kepler derive the laws of planetary motion.

He came to Prague in 1599 as Emperor Rudolf II's official mathematician. But Brahe also dabbled in astrology and alchemy. He lost part of his nose in a duel and wore a metal replacement. His pet moose apparently drank too much beer, fell down the stairs and died.

In Prague, Brahe himself died in 1601 of a bladder infection, reputedly because he was too polite to go to the toilet during a long banquet. Only recently have historians decided he was probably poisoned instead. We're not sure which version is more comforting.

nightly jazz sessions. Bands play anything from trad New Orleans jazz to bebop, blues, funk and soul. (☎221 466 138; www.bluessklep.cz; Liliová 10; cover 100-150Kč; ☉bar 7pm-2.30am, music 9pm-midnight; 🚋2, 17, 18)

Shopping

Art Deco Galerie
ANTIQUES

21 🔒 Map p74, C3

Specialising in early-20th-century items, this shop has a wide range of 1920s and '30s stuff, including clothes, handbags, jewellery, glassware and ceramics, along with knick-knacks such as the kind of cigarette case you might imagine Dorothy Parker pulling out of her purse. (☎224 223 076; www.artdecogalerie-mili.com; Michalská 21; ☉2-7pm Mon-Fri, to 6pm Sat; 🇲Můstek)

Modernista
HOMEWARES

22 🔒 Map p74, E2

Modernista specialises in reproduction 20th-century furniture, ceramics, glassware and jewellery in classic styles ranging from art-deco and cubist to functionalist and Bauhaus. This branch, located in the Municipal House information centre, is strong on jewellery and ceramics; the main showroom, in **Vinohradský Pavilon** (Vinohradská tržnice; www.pavilon.cz; Vinohradská 50, Vinohrady; ☉10am-7.30pm Mon-Fri, to 6pm Sat; 🇲Jiřího z Poděbrad, 🚋11, 13),

has sensuously curved chairs that are a feature of the Icon Hotel, and an unusual chaise lounge by Adolf Loos. (☎222 002 102; www.modernista.cz; náměstí Republiky 5, Municipal House; ☉10am-6pm; 🇲Náměstí Republiky)

Manufaktura
ARTS & CRAFTS

23 🔒 Map p74, C3

There are several Manufaktura outlets across town, but this small branch near Old Town Square seems to keep its inventory especially enticing. You'll find great Czech wooden toys, beautiful-looking (if extremely chewy) honey gingerbread made from elaborate medieval moulds, and seasonal gifts such as hand-painted Easter eggs. (☎601 310 611; www.manufaktura.cz; Melantrichova 17; ☉10am-8pm; 🇲Můstek)

Botanicus
COSMETICS

24 🔒 Map p74, D1

Prepare for olfactory overload in this always-busy outlet for natural health and beauty products. The scented soaps, herbal bath oils and shampoos, fruit cordials and handmade paper products are made using herbs and plants grown on an organic farm at Ostrá, east of Prague. (☎234 767 446; www.botanicus.cz; Týn 3; ☉10am-6.30pm Nov-Mar, to 8pm Apr-Oct; 🇲Náměstí Republiky)

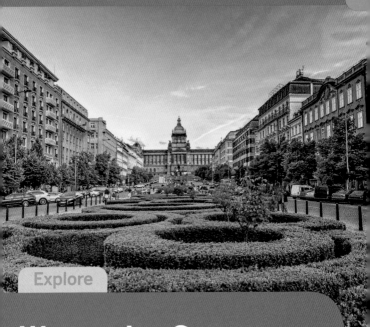

Explore

Wenceslas Square & Around

Busy Wenceslas Square, dating from 1348 and once a bustling horse market, was the site of several seminal events in Czech history. Today, though, it's crowded with souvenir shops, clubs, coffee chains and plenty of tourists, it's possible to glimpse the square's previous grandeur simply by looking up at the glorious art nouveau architecture.

The Sights in a Day

☀ Start the day at the bottom of **Wenceslas Square** (p86), the most important part of Nové Město. The square is a hodgepodge of architectural styles, but the art nouveau facade of the **Grand Hotel Evropa** (p87), at No 25, stands out. Walk up the square at your leisure, popping in at the **Hotel Jalta** (p89) to see an underground nuclear bunker. Check out the **Wenceslas Statue** (p87), the square's focal point. The National Museum is closed for renovation, but you can still take in the view, and also pay your respects at the **Jan Palach Memorial** (p87) and gaze over at the former headquarters of **Radio Free Europe** (p87).

☀ For lunch, head north of the square for standard pub fare at **U Ferdinanda** (p91), which then puts you within easy walking distance for the **Mucha Museum** (p89) to admire the painter's dreamlike beauties emblazoned on early-20th-century Parisian posters.

☾ For dinner, try some amazing tapas at **Room** (p90) or go totally casual for ribs and a Czech regional beer at **Jáma** (p92). If you want something lighter, try **Styl & Interier** (p91) and then a night of ballet or opera at the **Prague State Opera** (p93).

👁 **Top Sights**

Wenceslas Square (p86)

💜 **Best of Prague**

Food
Room (p90)

Styl & Interier (p91)

Museums
Mucha Museum (p89)

Museum of Communism (p90)

Architecture
Grand Hotel Evropa (p87)

Shopping
Moser (p95)

Baťa (p93)

Culture
Prague State Opera (p93)

Kino Světozor (p93)

Nighlife
Lucerna Music Bar (p92)

Getting There

Ⓜ **Metro** Lines A and B cross at Můstek at the bottom of the square. Lines A and C meet at Muzeum at the top.

Top Sights
Wenceslas Square

This massive central square was founded by
Charles IV in 1348. For hundreds of years it was
called the 'Horse Market' and featured a small
lake, horse-drawn trams and the first Czech
theatre. In medieval times it was also the site of
several public executions. On 28 October 1918,
the independent republic of Czechoslovakia was
announced here; in 1945 the end of WWII was
declared and celebrated. Later, during the Velvet
Revolution, the square hosted huge, historic
demonstrations.

Václavské náměstí

◉ Map p88, C3

Ⓜ Můstek, Muzeum

St Wenceslas statue

Jan Palach Memorial

In January 1969 university student Jan Palach set fire to himself in front of the National Museum to protest against the Soviet-led invasion of Czechoslovakia the preceding August. Palach later died from his wounds and became a national hero. The **memorial** (Václavské náměstí 68; ⏰24hr; MMuzeum) sits at the exact spot where Palach fell, marked by a cross in the pavement just below the steps to the museum's entrance.

Former Radio Free Europe Building

During the Cold War, many Czechs and Slovaks turned to US-financed Radio Free Europe for news from the West. After 1989, the radio moved its headquarters from Munich here to the former Czechoslovak Federal Parliament building (at the top of the square, just to the left of the National Museum). In 2008, RFE moved to a new building in the Prague suburbs, and the **old headquarters** (📞224 497 111; www.nm.cz; Vinohradská 1; adult/child 200/140Kč; ⏰10am-6pm; MMuzeum) is now used as a National Museum annex.

St Wenceslas Statue

The focal point of Wenceslas Sq is the equestrian statue of **St Wenceslas** (sv Václav; Václavské náměstí; MMuzeum) at its southern end. Sculptor Josef Myslbek has surrounded the 10th-century Duke of Bohemia (and 'Good King Wenceslas' of Christmas-carol fame) with four other patron saints of Bohemia – Prokop, Adalbert, Agnes and Ludmila.

Grand Hotel Evropa

Grand indeed – this ornate **art nouveau hotel** (Václavské náměstí 25) and cafe at Václavské náměstí 25 is easily the most colourful building on a colourful square. Unfortunately, it was closed for renovation at the time of research and it wasn't clear when it would reopen.

☑ Top Tips

▶ During holidays and festivals, try the square's food and drink stands for local specialties like spiced wine and grilled sausage.

▶ Keep an eye on your belongings, especially at night – this area is notorious for pickpockets and touts.

▶ Many restaurants on the square are tourist traps; better-value options are nearby.

✗ Take a Break

To escape the throngs, dive into the Lucerna shopping passage on Wenceslas Sq's southern side (enter from either Vodičkova or Štěpánská). Try **Kavárna Lucerna** (📞224 215 495; www.restaurace-monarchie.cz/en/cafe-lucerna; Pasáž Lucerna, Štěpánská 61; ⏰10am-midnight; 🛜; 🚋3, 5, 6, 9, 14, 24), on the upper floor, and the student favourite, **Kávovarna** (📞296 236 233; www.facebook.com/kavovarna; Pasáž Lucerna, Štěpánská 61; ⏰9am-11pm Mon-Fri, 2-11pm Sat, 2-10.30pm Sun; 🚋3, 5, 6, 9, 14, 24), on the ground floor.

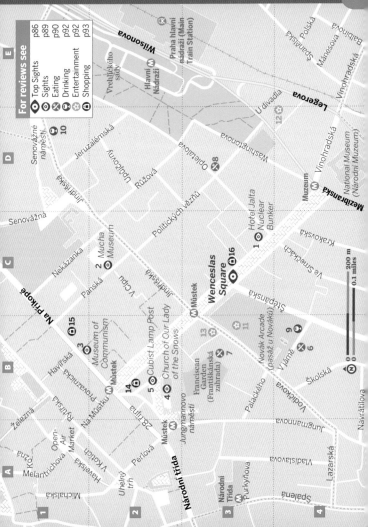

Praha hlavní nádraží (Main Train Station)

Wilsonova

Vrchlického sady

Hlavní Nádraží

Senovážné náměstí

Jeruzalémská

Jindřišská

Senovážná

Mucha Museum

Úpijčíkova

Růžová

Opletalova

Washingtonova

Politických vězňů

U divadla

Legerova

Vinohradská

National Museum (Národní Muzeum)

Muzeum

Mezibranská

Hotel Jalta

Nuclear Bunker

Wenceslas Square

Mústek

Na Příkopě

Nekázanka

Panská

V cípu

Jindřišská

Ve Smečkách

Krakovská

Štěpánská

200 m
0.1 miles

Museum of Communism

Havířská

Provaznická

Rytířská

Mústek

Cubist Lamp Post

Church of Our Lady of the Snows

Franciscan Garden (Františkánská zahrada)

Novák Arcade (pasáž u Nováků)

V Jámě

Palackého

Vodičkova

Jungmannova

Školská

Železná

Open-Air Market

Melantrichova

Havelská

V Kotcích

Na Mústku

Kožná

Michalská

Uhelný trh

Perlova

28. října

Jungmannovo náměstí

Národní třída

Národní Třída

Purkyňova

Vladislavova

Lazarská

Spálená

Vlašská

Navrátilova

Balbínova

Španělská

Mánesova

Polská

Vinohradská

Sights

Hotel Jalta Nuclear Bunker
HISTORIC BUILDING

1 Map p88, C3

Hidden beneath the 1950s Hotel Jalta on Wenceslas Square lies a communist-era nuclear shelter that was opened to the public in 2013. The tour, led by a guide in period security police uniform, takes in a series of secret chambers; the highlight is the comms room, where wiretaps in the bedrooms of important guests were monitored. (☎222 822 111; www.hotel jalta.com; Václavské náměstí 45; adult/child 120/60Kč; ☉tours in English 2-7pm Fri-Sun; Ⓜ Můstek, Muzeum)

Mucha Museum
GALLERY

2 Map p88, C2

This fascinating (and busy) museum features the sensuous art-nouveau posters, paintings and decorative panels of Alfons Mucha (1860–1939), as well as many sketches, photographs and other memorabilia. The exhibits include countless artworks showing Mucha's trademark Slavic maidens with flowing hair and piercing blue eyes, bearing symbolic garlands and linden boughs. (Muchovo muzeum; ☎221 451 333; www.mucha.cz; Panská 7; adult/child 240/160Kč; ☉10am-6pm; 🚋3, 5, 6, 9, 14, 24)

Understand
Much Ado About Mucha

Alfons Mucha (1860–1939) is the Czech answer to Austria's Gustav Klimt, England's William Morris or Scotland's Charles Rennie Mackintosh.

One of the fathers – if not *the* father – of art nouveau as represented in the visual arts, he first found fame in Paris after producing a stunning poster for actress Sarah Bernhardt's 1895 play *Gismonda*. A contract with Bernhardt, reams of advertising work and trips to America brought him international renown.

Mucha returned home in 1909, and went on to design the banknotes for the first Czechoslovak Republic after 1918. Around this time, he also produced his opus, a collection of 20 gigantic canvases telling the history of the Slavic peoples, which he titled the *Slav Epic (Slovanská epopej)*.

Mucha created some of the stunning interiors of Prague's Municipal House (p75) and designed a beautiful stained-glass window for St Vitus Cathedral (p30). His signature art nouveau work is on display at the Mucha Museum (p89).

Long-held plans to exhibit the *Slav Epic* in Prague came to fruition in 2013, when the canvases were put on display at the National Gallery's Veletržní Palác (p120); they're slated to stay through at least 2015.

Cubist Lamp Post

Church of Our Lady of the Snows

CHURCH

 4 Map p88, B2

This Gothic church at the northern end of Wenceslas Square was begun in the 14th century by Charles IV, but only the chancel was ever completed, which accounts for its proportions – seemingly taller than it is long. Charles had intended it to be the grandest church in Prague; the nave is higher than that of St Vitus Cathedral, and the altar is the city's tallest. (Kostel Panny Marie Sněžné; www.pms.ofm.cz; Jungmannovo náměstí 18; MMůstek)

Cubist Lamp Post

PUBLIC ART

 5 Map p88, B2

Angular but slightly chunky, made from striated concrete – the world's only cubist lamp post would be worth going out of the way to see. So it's a happy bonus that this novelty is just around the corner from Wenceslas Square. (Jungmannovo náměstí; MMůstek)

Museum of Communism

MUSEUM

 3 Map p88, B1

It's difficult to think of a more ironic site for a museum of communism – in an 18th-century aristocrat's palace, between a casino on one side and a McDonald's on the other. Put together by an American expat and his Czech partner, the museum tells the story of Czechoslovakia's years behind the Iron Curtain in photos, words and a fascinating and varied collection of... well, stuff. (Muzeum Komunismu; ☏224 212 966; www.muzeumkomunismu.cz; Na příkopě 10; adult/child under 10yr 190Kč/free; ◷9am-9pm; MMůstek)

Eating

Room

SPANISH $$

 6 Map p88, B4

Cool, angular and precise in shades of grey, black and avocado green, Room provides the perfect setting for some of Prague's most carefully crafted flavours. With an accomplished kitchen team working from a menu created by actor Tommy Lee Jones's personal chef, it's no surprise that the

Understand
Overhaul of the National Museum

The National Museum, at the top end of the square, dates from the last half of the 19th century, when bombastic architecture was all the rage. The style, neo-Renaissance, was meant as a conscious aping of the Renaissance palaces that were built around Prague in the 16th century. The grand size served two purposes: the museum's vast holdings could finally fit under one roof, and the building was meant to symbolise the power of the growing Czech (as opposed to Austrian or German) elite.

As this book was being researched, the museum was undergoing long-term renovation – until 2018 at the earliest. The repairs are meant to spruce up the facade (which was still sporting bullet holes from 1968, when it was fired on by invading Russian troops who mistook it for Parliament) and to modernise the fusty exhibits of fossils, rocks and bones. During the renovation, the museum is organising temporary exhibits next door at the National Museum's new building.

food – *gambas pil pil,* Argentinian beef skewers, grilled octopus with fava beans – is top-notch. (☎221 634 103; www.tapasroom.cz; V Jámě 6, Icon Hotel; tapas 80-250Kc; ⏱bar 7am-1am, tapas 11am-11pm; ☎; ☒3, 5, 6, 9, 14, 24)

Styl & Interier
CAFE $

7 ✗ Map p88, B3

A passage opposite the Vodičkova entrance to the Lucerna Palace leads to this secret retreat, a rustic cafe with a high-walled garden where local shoppers gather in wicker armchairs beneath the trees to enjoy coffee and cake, or a lunch of lasagne, quiche and salad, or slow-cooked lamb with red wine gravy. Best to book a table. (☎222 543 128; www.stylainterier.cz/kavarna; Vodičkova 35; mains 100-200Kč; ⏱9.30am-9pm Mon-Sat, to 8pm Sun; ☎; ☒3, 5, 6, 9, 14, 24)

U Ferdinanda
CZECH $

8 ✗ Map p88, D3

Welcome to a thoroughly modern spin on a classic Czech pub with beer courtesy of the Ferdinand brewery from nearby Benešov. Quirky gardening implements in corrugated iron decorate the raucous interior, and a younger local clientele crowds in for well-prepared and well-priced traditional Czech food. (☎775 135 575; www.ferdinanda.cz; cnr ulice Opletalova & Politických Vězňů; mains 150-250Kč; ⏱11am-11pm Mon-Sat; Ⓜ Muzeum)

> ## Understand
> ### Prague's Grand Cafes
>
> Prague is known for pubs, Vienna for its coffeehouses. Yet the Czech capital also boasts grand cafes that rival their Austrian cousins in looks (even if the actual coffee can't compete). At least the atmosphere is equivalent, and since the days of the Austro-Hungarian Empire onwards, Prague's ornate, high-ceilinged coffeehouses have acted as public meeting spaces, hotbeds of political subversion and literary salons.
>
> At various times Franz Kafka, playwright Karel Čapek (coiner of the term 'robot') and Albert Einstein all drank at Cafe Louvre (p101), while across the road at Kavárna Slavia (p101), patrons included Milan Kundera, Václav Havel and other writers, playwrights and filmmakers.

Drinking

Jáma   BAR

9 Map p88, B4

Jáma ('the Hollow') is a popular American-expat bar plastered with old rock-gig posters ranging from Led Zep and REM to Kiss and Shania Twain. There's a little beer garden out the back shaded by lime and walnut trees, smiling staff serving up a rotating selection of regional beers and microbrews, and a menu that includes good burgers, steaks, ribs and chicken wings. (☑222 967 081; www.jamapub.cz; V Jámě 7; ☉11am-1am Tue-Sun, to midnight Mon; ☎; ☐3, 5, 6, 9, 14, 24)

Hoffa   COCKTAIL BAR

10 Map p88, D1

One of Prague's first entirely smoke-free bars, Hoffa matches clean air with clean design: a long (12m long!) bar fronts a room with sleek, functional decor and a wall of windows looking out onto Senovážné náměstí's fountain of dancing sprites. Friendly staff, accomplished cocktails and good food – you'll be struggling to find a table at lunchtime. (☑601 359 659; www.hoffa.cz; Senovážné náměstí 22; ☉11am-2am Mon-Fri, 6pm-2am Sat, 6pm-midnight Sun; ☎; ☐3, 5, 6, 9, 14, 24)

Entertainment

Lucerna Music Bar   LIVE MUSIC

11 ⭐ Map p88, B3

Nostalgia reigns supreme at this atmospheric old theatre, now looking a little dog-eared. It hosts a hugely popular 1980s and '90s video party from 9pm every Friday and Saturday night, with crowds of young locals bopping along to Duran Duran and Gary Numan. (☑224 217 108; www.musicbar.cz; Palác Lucerna, Vodičkova 36; cover 100-500Kč; ☉hours vary; M Můstek)

Museum of Communism (p90)

Prague State Opera
OPERA, BALLET

12 ⭐ Map p88, D4

The impressive neo-rococo home of the Prague State Opera provides a glorious setting for performances of opera and ballet. The building is closed for renovation work until 2018. (Státní opera Praha; 📞224 901 448; www.narodni-divadlo.cz; Wilsonova 4; ⏰box office 10am-6pm; Ⓜ Muzeum)

Kino Světozor
CINEMA

13 ⭐ Map p88, B3

The Světozor is under the same management as Žižkov's famous **Kino Aero** (📞271 771 349; www.kinoaero.cz; Biskupcova 31, Žižkov; tickets 60-120Kč; 📶; 🚊1, 9, 10,

11, 16), but is more central, and has the same emphasis on classic cinema, documentary and art-house films screened in their original language – everything from *Battleship Potemkin* and *Casablanca* to *Annie Hall* and *The Motorcycle Diaries* – plus critically acclaimed box office hits. (📞224 946 824; www.kinosvetozor.cz; Vodičkova 41; tickets 60-120Kč; 📶; Ⓜ Můstek)

Shopping

Baťa
SHOES

14 🔒 Map p88, B2

Established by Tomáš Baťa in 1894, the Baťa footwear empire is still in

Understand

Oppression & Revolution

From Coup to Invasion

February 1948 marked the start of a half-century's worth of political turmoil in Prague. It was at this time that the leaders of the Czechoslovak Communist Party (KSČ), not content with a controlling position in the postwar coalition after the 1946 elections, staged a coup d'état backed by the Soviet Union. The next two decades saw widespread political persecution.

In the late 1960s, Communist Party leader Alexander Dubček loosened the reins slightly under the banner 'Socialism With a Human Face'. There was a resurgence in literature, theatre and film, led by the likes of Milan Kundera, Bohumil Hrabal, Václav Havel and Miloš Forman. The Soviet regime crushed this 'Prague Spring' on 20 and 21 August 1968, using Warsaw Pact tanks, and Dubček was replaced by hardliner Gustáv Husák.

The Fall of Communism

The Husák government expelled many reform communists from positions of authority and introduced what Czechs called 'normalisation' – in other words, Soviet-style repression. Active dissent was limited to a few hundred people, mostly intellectuals and artists, including playwright Václav Havel.

In November 1989, as communist regimes tumbled across Eastern Europe, the Czechoslovak government came under increasing pressure to relinquish power. On 17 November, riot police cracked down on a peaceful student protest march, which would prove to be the catalyst to revolution. Within days, crowds on Wenceslas Square swelled to some 500,000 people.

A group led by Havel procured the government's resignation on 3 December, and 26 days later, he was the new leader. The 'Velvet Revolution' – named for its peaceful nature (as well as the inspiration its leaders took from the rock band the Velvet Underground) – had triumphed.

A Velvet Divorce

The transition to democracy was anything but smooth, though it eventually succeeded. Ironically, one casualty of the revolution was the splitting of the country into separate Czech and Slovak states in 1993. The amicable breakup later became known as the 'Velvet Divorce'.

family hands and is one of the Czech Republic's most successful companies. The flagship store on Wenceslas Square, built in the 1920s, is considered a masterpiece of modern architecture, and houses six floors of shoes (including international brands as well as Baťa's own), handbags, luggage and leather goods. (☑221 088 478; www. bata.cz; Václavské náměstí 6; ⊘9am-9pm Mon-Sat, 10am-9pm Sun; Ⓜ Můstek)

Moser   GLASS

15 🔒 Map p88, B1

One of the most exclusive and respected of Bohemian glassmakers, Moser was founded in Karlovy Vary in 1857 and is famous for its rich and flamboyant designs. The shop on Na Příkopě is worth a browse as much for the decor as for the goods – it's in a magnificently decorated, originally Gothic building called the House of the Black Rose (dům U černé růže). (☑224 211 293; www.moser-glass.com; Na příkopě 12; ⊘10am-8pm Mon-Fri, to 7pm Sat & Sun; Ⓜ Můstek)

Palác Knih Neo Luxor   BOOKS

16 🔒 Map p88, C3

Palác Knih Neo Luxor is Prague's biggest bookshop – head for the basement to find a wide selection of fiction

🔍 Local Life

Shopping 'At the Moat'

Crossing the lower end of Wenceslas Square, Na Příkopě is one of the city's prettiest and most popular promenades. The name translates as 'At the Moat' – the street traces a moat that once ran between Staré Město and Nové Město to protect the Old Town from attack.

In the 19th century, Na Příkopě was the fashionable haunt of Austrian cafe society. Today, it's typical high-street shopping turf, lined with international retail chains like H&M, Mango and Zara, and dotted with colourful shopping malls, including dům U černé růže (House of the Black Rose) at No 12, Myslbek pasáž (www.myslbek.com) at No 21, Slovanský dům at No 22, and Palladium (www.palladiumpraha. cz) at náměstí Republiky 1.

and nonfiction in English, German, French and Russian, including Czech authors in translation. You'll also find internet access, a cafe and a good selection of international newspapers and magazines. (☑296 110 368; www.neo luxor.cz; Václavské náměstí 41; ⊘8am-8pm Mon-Fri, 9am-7pm Sat, 10am-7pm Sun; 🚊3, 5, 6, 9, 14, 24)

Explore

Nové Město

Nové Město is a long, arching neighbourhood that borders Staré Město on its eastern and southern edges. The name translates as 'New Town', which is something of a misnomer since the area was established nearly 700 years ago by Emperor Charles IV. But unlike Staré Město or Malá Strana, the historic feeling is missing here, owing mainly to massive reconstruction in the 19th century.

The Sights in a Day

Start your day with a cup of coffee at **Kavárna Slavia** (p101) – try to snag a river-facing table with a view to Prague Castle. Meander down by the river, heading south to **Slav Island** (p99), where you can rent a paddle boat and enjoy a terrific, water-level view of CharleMaso a Koblihas Bridge. From here, wander further south to take in the **Dancing House** (p99), one of the few modern buildings in Prague to make a splash in architectural circles. From there, head east to the **Church of Sts Cyril & Methodius** (p100), the site of a dramatic stand-off between the Nazis and a band of brave Czechoslovak paratroopers during World War II.

Follow Na Zderace north to a quieter part of town, the area south of Národní třída. Grab a spicy Thai lunch at **Lemon Leaf** (p100) or soup and sandwich combo at the **Globe Bookstore & Cafe** (p100).

In the evening get tickets to see a ballet or opera at the beautiful **National Theatre** (pictured left; p101) or enjoy a jazz set at **Reduta** (p102). Kids will enjoy a night of 'black theatre' at **Laterna Magika** (p102). **Cafe Louvre** (p101), though technically a coffee house, is a terrific choice for a stylish Czech dinner.

💜 Best of Nové Město

Food
Cafe Louvre (p101)

Lemon Leaf (p100)

History
National Memorial to the Heroes of the Heydrich Terror (p100)

Architecture
Dancing House (p99)

Culture
National Theatre (p101)

Laterna Magika (p102)

Drinking
Cafe Louvre (p101)

Kavárna Slavia (p101)

Pivovarský Dům (p101)

Music
Reduta Jazz Club (p102)

Getting There

Ⓜ **Metro** Line B to Můstek or Karlovo Náměstí; Line A to Můstek

🚋 **Tram** Trams 6, 9, 17, 18, 22 to Národní divadlo

200 m
0.1 miles

Wenceslas Square (Václavské náměstí)

Muzeum Ⓜ

Mezibranská

Czech Blind United

Krakovská

Ve Smečkách

For reviews see

Ⓞ	Sights	p99
⊗	Eating	p100
◉	Drinking	p101
⊗	Entertainment	p101
◉	Shopping	p103

IP Pavlova

Mústek Ⓜ

Lucerna Palace (Palác Lucerna)

Štěpánská

Ječná

Na Rybníčku II

Jungmannovo náměstí

Franciscan Garden (Františkánská zahrada)

Palackého

Vodičkova

Školská

Vejárna

Jungmannova

Navrátilova

Řeznická

Žitná

Povl

8

Mústek Ⓜ

Adria Palace

Vladislavova

Lazarská

Příčná

Malá Štěpánská

Národní Třída Ⓜ

Purkyňova

Spálená

Charles Square (Karlovo náměstí)

Na Perštýně

12

Mikulandská

10 5

14

Voršilská

Ostrovní

V Jirchářích

Opatovická

Černá

Odborů

NOVÉ MĚSTO

Karlovo Náměstí Ⓜ

Vyšehradská

Charles Square (Karlovo náměstí)

Bartolomějská

7

Křemencová

3

Myslíkova

4

Na Zderaze

NOVÉ MĚSTO

Václavská

Resslova

Dittrichov

Konviktská

Národní třída

Pštrossova

Nástruze

Vojtěšská

Šítkova

Zborovská

Jiráskovo náměstí

Dancing House

Divadelní

6

11

9

Masarykovo nábřeží

1

Smetanovo nábřeží

Slav Island

Slav Island (Slovanský ostrov)

2

Jiráskův most (Jiráskův most)

13

Jiráskův Bridge (Jiráskův most)

Jirásek Square (Jiráskovo náměstí)

Dancing House

Sights

Dancing House ARCHITECTURE

1 🎯 Map p98, A4

The Dancing House was built in 1996 by architects Vlado Milunić and Frank Gehry. The curved lines of the narrow-waisted glass tower clutched against its more upright and formal partner led to it being christened the 'Fred & Ginger' building, after legendary dancing duo Fred Astaire and Ginger Rogers. It's surprising how well it fits in with its ageing neighbours. (Tančící dům; http://tadu.cz; Rašínovo nábřeží 80; 🚋 5, 17)

Slav Island ISLAND

2 🎯 Map p98, A2

This island is a sleepy, dog-eared sandbank with pleasant gardens, river views and several jetties where you can hire rowing boats. In the middle stands **Žofín**, a 19th-century cultural centre that has been restored as a restaurant and social venue. In 1925 the island was named after the Slav conventions that had taken place here since 1848. (Slovanský ostrov; Masarykovo nábřeží; 🚋 5, 17)

Understand
Heroic Paratroopers

- -

In 1941, during WWII, the occupying Nazi government appointed SS general Reinhard Heydrich, Hitler's heir apparent, as Reichsprotektor of Bohemia and Moravia. The move came in response to a series of crippling strikes and sabotage operations by the Czech resistance movement, and Heydrich immediately cracked down with a vengeance.

In an effort to support the resistance and boost Czech morale, Britain secretly trained a team of Czechoslovak paratroopers to assassinate Heydrich. The daring mission was code-named 'Operation Anthropoid' – and against all odds it succeeded. On 27 May 1942, two paratroopers, Jan Kubiš and Jozef Gabčík, attacked Heydrich as he rode in his official car through the city's Libeň district; he later died from the wounds.

The assassins and five co-conspirators fled but were betrayed in their hiding place in the Church of Sts Cyril & Methodius; all seven died in the ensuing siege. This moving story is told at the **National Memorial to the Heroes of the Heydrich Terror** (Národní památník hrdinů Heydrichiády; ☑ 224 916 100; www.pamatnik-heydrichiady.cz; Resslova 9; admission free; ⊙ 9am-5pm Tue-Sun Mar-Oct, 9am-5pm Tue-Sat Nov-Feb; Ⓜ Karlovo Náměstí) located at the church.

The Nazis reacted with a frenzied wave of terror, which included the annihilation of two entire Czech villages, Ležáky and Lidice, and the shattering of the underground movement.

Eating

Globe Bookstore & Café   CAFE €

3 Map p98, B3

This appealing expat bookshop-cafe serves nachos, burgers, chicken wings and salads until 11pm nightly, and also offers an excellent brunch menu (9.30am to 3pm Saturday and Sunday) that includes an American classic (bacon, egg and hash browns), full English fry-up, blueberry pancakes and freshly squeezed juices. Lighter breakfasts are served from 10am to noon weekdays.

(☑ 224 934 203; www.globebookstore.cz; Pštrossova 6; mains 150-300Kč; ⊙ 10am-11pm; 🛜; Ⓜ Karlovo Náměstí)

Lemon Leaf   ASIAN €€

4 Map p98, B3

It's a bit off the beaten tourist path, but with its high-ceilinged rooms, atmospheric lighting and arty photographs, the Lemon Leaf is certainly making an effort to pull in the visitors. And it's worth a visit for excellent, authentic Thai dishes, including a rich and fragrant green curry with a decent kick of chilli heat. (☑ 224 919 056; www.lemon.cz;

Myslíkova 14; mains 160-240Kč; ⏰11am-11pm
Mon-Fri, noon-11pm Sat & Sun; 📶; 🚋5)

Drinking

Cafe Louvre   CAFE

 5   Map p98, B1

The French-style Cafe Louvre is argu-
ably the most amenable of Prague's
grand cafes, as popular today as it
was in the early 1900s when it was
frequented by the likes of Franz Kafka
and Albert Einstein. The atmosphere
is wonderfully olde-worlde, and it
serves good food as well as coffee.
Check out the billiard hall, and the
ground-floor art gallery. (📞224 930
949; www.cafelouvre.cz; 1st fl, Národní třída
22; ⏰8am-11.30pm Mon-Fri, 9am-11.30pm
Sat & Sun; 🚋2, 9, 18, 22)

Kavárna Slavia   CAFE

6   Map p98, A1

The Slavia is the most famous of
Prague's old cafes, a cherrywood-and-
onyx shrine to art-deco elegance, with
polished limestone-topped tables and
big windows overlooking the river. It
has been a celebrated literary meeting
place since the early 20th century –
Rainer Maria Rilke and Franz Kafka
hung out here, and it was frequented
by Václav Havel and other dissidents
in the 1970s and '80s. (📞224 220 957;
www.cafeslavia.cz; Národní třída 1; ⏰8am-
midnight Mon-Fri, 9am-midnight Sat & Sun;
📶; 🚋2, 9, 18, 22)

U Fleků   BREWERY

 7   Map p98, B3

A festive warren of drinking and
dining rooms, U Fleků is a Prague institution, although it's usually clogged
with tour groups high on oompah
music and the tavern's home-brewed,
13-degree black beer (59Kč for 0.4L),
known as Flek. Purists grumble but go
along anyway because the beer is good,
though tourist prices have nudged out
many locals. (📞224 934 019; www.ufleku.
cz; Křemencová 11; ⏰10am-11pm; 🚋5)

Pivovarský Dům   BREWERY

 8   Map p98, D4

While the tourists flock to U Fleků
(p101), locals gather here to sample
the Štěpán classic Czech lager (44Kč
per 0.5L) that is produced on the
premises, as well as wheat beer and
a range of flavoured beers (including
coffee, banana and cherry; 44Kč per
0.3L). The pub itself, decked out with
polished copper vats and brewing
implements, is a pleasant place to
linger. (📞296 216 666; www.pivovarskydum.
com; cnr Ječná & Lípová; ⏰11am-11.30pm;
🚋4, 6, 10, 16, 22)

Entertainment

National Theatre   OPERA, BALLET

9   Map p98, A2

The much-loved National Theatre provides a stage for traditional opera, drama and ballet by the likes of Smetana,
Shakespeare and Tchaikovsky, sharing

Local Life
South of Národní Třída

The area south of Národní třída, behind the National Theatre, is lined with lesser-known ethnic eateries, student-populated cafes, and (lots of) bars. It's a lovely part of town to wander along as the sun fades. Come back after dark, since this is one of the better places to party.

Red Room (📞602 429 989; www.redroom.cz; Myslíkova 28; ⏰5pm-3am Sun-Thu, to 5am Fri & Sat; 📶; 🚊5) Laid-back bar stuffed with friendly expats and offering occasional live music.

Kavárna Velryba (📞224 931 444; www.kavarnavelryba.cz; Opatovická 24; ⏰11am-11pm Mon-Fri, noon-11pm Sat & Sun; 📶; 🚊2, 9, 18, 22) Arty cafe-bar with vegetarian-friendly snacks, a smoky back room and a basement art gallery.

the program alongside more modern works by composers and playwrights such as Philip Glass and John Osborne. The box offices are in the Nový síň building next door, in the Kolowrat Palace (opposite the Estates Theatre) and at the State Opera. (Národní divadlo; 📞224 901 448; www.narodni-divadlo.cz; Národní třída 2; tickets 100-1290Kč; ⏰box offices 10am-6pm; 🚊2, 9, 18, 22)

Reduta Jazz Club   JAZZ

10 ⭐ Map p98, B1

The Reduta is Prague's oldest jazz club, founded in 1958 during the com-

munist era – it was here in 1994 that former US president Bill Clinton famously jammed on a new saxophone presented to him by Václav Havel. It has an intimate setting, with smartly dressed patrons squeezing into tiered seats and lounges to soak up the big-band, swing and Dixieland atmosphere. (📞224 933 487; www.redutajazzclub.cz; Národní třída 20; cover 330-490Kč; ⏰9pm-3am; 📶; Ⓜ Národní Třída)

Laterna Magika   PERFORMING ARTS

11 ⭐ Map p98, A2

Laterna Magika has been wowing audiences since its first cutting-edge multimedia show caused a stir at the 1958 Brussels World Fair. Its imaginative blend of dance, music and projected images continues to pull in the crowds. Nová Scena, the futuristic building next to the National Theatre, has been home to Laterna Magika since it moved here from its birthplace in the Adria Palace in the mid-1970s. (📞224 901 417; www.narodni-divadlo.cz; Nová Scéna, Národní třída 4; tickets 260-690Kč; ⏰box office 9am-6pm Mon-Fri, 10am-6pm Sat & Sun; 🚊2, 9, 18, 22)

Image Theatre   PERFORMING ARTS

12 ⭐ Map p98, B1

Founded in 1989, this company uses creative black-light theatre along with pantomime, modern dance and video – not to mention liberal doses of slapstick – to tell its stories. The staging can be very effective, but the atmosphere is often dictated by audience reaction. (Divadlo Image; 📞222

FLORIN DRAGHICI/500PX ©

Náplavka Farmers Market

314 448; www.imagetheatre.cz; Národní 25; tickets 480Kč; ⊙box office 10am-8pm; MStaroměstská)

Shopping

Náplavka Farmers Market

MARKET

13 🔒 Map p98, A4

Stretching along the embankment from Trojická to Výton, this weekly market makes the most of its riverside setting with live music and outdoor tables scattered among stalls selling freshly baked bread, organic locally grown vegetables, homemade cakes and pastries, wild mushrooms (in season), herbs, flowers, wild honey, hot food, Czech cider, coffee and a range of arts and crafts. (www.farmarsketrziste. cz; Rašínovo nábřeží; ⊙8am-2pm Sat; 🚊2, 3, 7, 17, 21)

Belda Jewellery

JEWELLERY

14 🔒 Map p98, B1

Belda & Co is a long-established Czech firm dating from 1922. Nationalised in 1948, it was revived by the founder's son and grandson, and continues to create gold and silver jewellery of a very high standard. Its range includes its own angular, contemporary designs, as well as reproductions based on art-nouveau designs by Alfons Mucha. (📞224 933 052; www.belda.cz; Mikulandská 10; ⊙11am-6pm Mon-Fri; MNárodní Třída)

Local Life
Vyšehrad, Prague's Other Castle

Getting There

Vyšehrad is located high above the banks of the Vltava River, just south of Nové Město.

Ⓜ Line C to Vyšehrad.

🚊 Lines 7, 14, 18 & 24 to Ostrčilovo náměstí.

The complex of buildings that make up **Vyšehrad Citadel** has played an important role in Czech history for more than a thousand years. While not many of the ancient buildings have survived to the present (most structures date from the 18th century, when the site was used as a fortress), the citadel is still viewed as Prague's spiritual home. For more information and an events calendar, see www.praha-vysehrad.cz.

❶ Through the Old Gates
Heading west, about 10 minutes on foot from the Vyšehrad metro station, you'll pass **Tábor Gate** and the remains of the original Gothic **Špička Gate**.

❷ Prague's Oldest Building
The 11th-century Romanesque **Rotunda of St Martin** is considered Prague's oldest surviving building. The door and frescos date from a renovation made in about 1880. It's normally closed, but the interior can be viewed during mass (times are posted at the door).

❸ Into the Fortress
Through the **Brick Gate & Casements** (adult/child 60/30Kč; ⏱9.30am-6pm Apr-Oct, to 5pm Nov-Mar) are hidden vaults once used for imprisonment and storing weapons when Vyšehrad served as a fortress in the 18th century. The underground **Gorlice Hall** holds some of the Charles Bridge's original statues.

❹ Outdoor Entertainment
If you're there in the warmer months, look out for musical performances and shows at Vyšehrad's open-air theatre, the **Summer Stage** (performances 300-700Kč; ⏱box office 5.30-8pm Apr-Oct).

❺ Dvořák's Final Resting Place
The 600 graves (many with intricately designed headstones) in the lovely gardens of **Vyšehrad Cemetery** (Vyšehradský hřbitov; ☎274 774 835; www.praha-vysehrad.cz; K Rotundě 10, Vyšehrad; admission free; ⏱8am-7pm May-Sep, shorter hours Oct-Apr; Ⓜ Vyšehrad) read like a who's who of

Czech arts and letters, including musicians Antonín Dvořák and Bedřich Smetana and artist Alfons Mucha.

❻ Last Church Standing
The neo-Gothic **Church of Sts Peter & Paul** (Kostel sv Petra a Pavla; ☎261 225 304; K Rotundé 10, Vyšehrad; adult/child 30/10Kč; ⏱9am-noon & 1-5pm Wed-Mon) was one of Vyšehrad's few structures to avoid destruction in 1420 during the Hussite religious wars. The current facade dates from the 19th century.

❼ Dinner While You're Here
Stop for a meal at **Rio's Vyšehrad** (www.riorestaurant.cz; Štulcova 2, Vyšehrad; mains 250-600Kč; ⏱10am-midnight), a classy Mediterranean restaurant featuring excellent fish dishes. Dine on the terrace in nice weather.

❽ Underground History
The atmospheric **Gothic Cellar** (adult/child 60/30Kč; ⏱9.30am-6pm Apr-Oct, to 5pm Nov-Mar) houses a worthwhile exhibit; its overview of the history of Prague's fortification helps put Vyšehrad's sights into perspective.

❾ Beer with a View
Along the fortress's southern ramparts, **Cafe Citadela** (⏱9.30am-6pm Apr-Sep, 10am-5pm Wed-Sun Oct-Mar) is an outdoor beer garden with a relaxed vibe and nice views. Come for a coffee or beer and enjoy the setting with a young, mostly local crowd.

Explore

Vinohrady & Žižkov

Vinohrady and Žižkov are the yin and yang of residential Prague. Gentrified Vinohrady, named for its days as the royal vineyards, boasts high-ceilinged, art nouveau apartment buildings and is popular with young professionals and expats. The 'people's republic' of Žižkov is historically working class, rebellious and revolutionary, famed for its numerous pubs, alternative nightlife and multicultural population.

The Sights in a Day

☼ Start your day with a coffee and pastry at one of the cafes around Peace Square (náměstí Míru), the centre of Vinohrady and easily reached by metro. We love **Bio Zahrada** (p115), a short walk from the square. Take the metro one stop to Jiřího z Poděbrad and admire the modern **Church of the Most Sacred Heart of Our Lord** (pictured left; p112). From here, it's just a short walk to the **TV Tower** (p112) in Žižkov, where you can ride to the top or simply ogle the larger-than-life baby statues crawling up the outside.

☼ There are lots of good lunch options in the area. Try **The Tavern** (p114) for burgers or down-to-earth Czech fare at **Pastička** (p115). If you get a sunny afternoon, relax at the neighborhood's **Riegrovy sady** (p113) park, where locals congregate for leisurely strolls and beer drinking.

☾ For evenings, try an elegant Italian dinner at **Aromi** (p113) or for some modern pub food head to **Vinohradský Parlament** (p108). Finish the day with some live music at **Palác Akropolis** (p116) or dancing at **Techtle Mechtle** (p117) or **Termix** (p109).

For a local's day in Vinohrady & Žižkov, see p108.

Local Life

Drinking Tour of Vinohrady & Žižkov (p108)

Best of Prague

Cafes & Pubs
U Slovanské Lípy (p116)

Bio Zahrada (p115)

Prague Beer Museum (p109)

Eating
Kofein (p114)

The Tavern (p114)

Nightlife
Palác Akropolis (p116)

Techtle Mechtle (p117)

Gay & Lesbian
Termix (p109)

Café Celebrity (p116)

Getting There

Ⓜ **Metro** Line A to Náměstí Míru, Jiřího z Poděbrad or Flora.

🚊 **Tram** Line 4, 10, 13, 16 or 22 to Náměstí Míru, line 11 or 13 to Jiřího z Poděbrad.

Local Life
Drinking Tour of Vinohrady & Žižkov

In Prague, there's no better place to make a night of it: Žižkov, on one side, proudly claims to have more pubs per square metre than anywhere else in the world; on the other side, classy Vinohrady is home to some serious wine and cocktail bars, where the staff really know how to mix a drink.

1 Line Your Stomach

A sturdy meal is always a good idea if a night of drinking is on the cards. **Vinohradský Parlament** (Map p110, B4; 224 250 403; www.vinohradskyparlament. cz; Korunní 1, Vinohrady; mains 180-250Kč; 11am-midnight Mon-Wed, to 1am Thu-Sat, 11.30am-11.30pm Sun; ; Náměstí Míru), on Peace Square (náměstí Míru), offers excellent modern twists on Czech pub food, paired with the best beers offered by the Staropramen brewery.

❷ Night at the 'Museum'

Just across Peace Square, the **Prague Beer Museum** (☎ reservations 775 994 698; www.praguebeermuseum.com; Americká 43, Vinohrady; ⏱ noon-3am; 🛜; Ⓜ Náměstí Míru) – actually a pub – offers 30 regional Czech beers on tap. So, once you've had your fill of Staropramen, see what else the country has to offer.

❸ French Wine With Style

One metro stop away, at Jiřího z Poděbrad, **Le Caveau** (☎ 775 294 864; www.broz-d.cz; náměstí Jiřího z Poděbrad 9, Vinohrady; ⏱ 8am-10.30pm Mon-Fri, 9am-10.30pm Sat, 2-8.30pm Sun; 🛜; Ⓜ Jiřího z Poděbrad) offers the city's best selection of French wines and upmarket cheeses and snacks to match. Wine-drinkers may want to start the night right here.

❹ Riegrovy Sady Beer Garden

A short walk from Jiřího z Poděbrad, the **Riegrovy Sady Beer Garden** (Riegrovy sady, Vinohrady; ⏱ noon-1am Apr-Oct; Ⓜ Jiřího z Poděbrad, 🚌 11, 13) is especially popular at night (until around 1am in summer), when the picnic tables fill to bursting with everyone making merry with cheap Gambrinus beer and slightly more expensive Pilsner Urquell.

❺ Classy Cocktails at Bar & Books

At this stage, you can stay classy or go crazy. For classy, **Bar & Books Mánesova** (☎ 222 724 581; www.barandbooks. cz; Mánesova 64, Vinohrady; ⏱ 5pm-3am Sun-Wed, to 4am Thu-Sat; 🛜; 🚌 11, 13) is a sensuous cocktail lounge featuring lush, library-themed decor, top-shelf liquor and live music some nights.

❻ Crazy Dancing at Termix

If crazy is the order of the night and it's after 10pm, gay-friendly **Termix** (Map p110, C4; ☎ 222 710 462; www. club-termix.cz; Trebízského 4a, Vinohrady; ⏱ 9pm-6am Wed-Sun; Ⓜ Jiřího z Poděbrad, 🚌 11, 13) is the place to spend the evening. It stays open until 5am or so on weekends, so no need to move on from here if this is your scene.

❼ Beer at U Sadu

For more working-class libations, the congenial neighbourhood pub **U Sadu** (☎ 222 727 072; www.usadu.cz; Škroupovo náměstí 5, Žižkov; ⏱ 8am-4am Tue-Sat, to 2am Sun & Mon; Ⓜ Jiřího z Poděbrad) is supremely popular with old locals, dreadlocked students and expats alike. Staff also run the kitchen past midnight here, so if you're craving a snack, this may be your only option.

❽ Nightcap at Bukowski's

On the Žižkov street that's reckoned to have more drinking dens per metre than anywhere else in Prague, **Bukowski's** (☎ 773 445 280; www.facebook. com/bukowskisbar; Bořivojova 86, Žižkov; ⏱ 7pm-3am; 🚌 5, 9, 15, 26), named after the hard-drinking American poet Charles Bukowski, is a cut above its neighbours. Expect cool tunes and confident cocktails.

NOVÉ MĚSTO

Náměstí Republiky

10

Na Florenci

Masarykovo nádraží

Hybernská

National Monument 4

Žižkov Hill

Senovážné náměstí

Husitská

Řehořova

Orebitská

Husinecká

Seifertova

Jindřišská

Opletalova

Wilsonova

PRAHA 1

U Rajské zahrady

FK Viktoria Žižkov Stadium

Vlkova

Krásova

Víta Nejedlého

Seifertova

Hlavní Nádraží

Praha hlavní nádraží (Main Train Station)

Růžová

Vrchlického sady

ŽIŽKOV

17

Former Jewish Cemetery

Rajská zahrada

Slavíkova

9

Kubelíkova

Fibichova

TV Tower

Washingtonova

Muzeum

Španělská

Helénská

Riegrovy sady

Na Švíhance

Křižíkovského

Škroupovo náměstí

2

Mahlerovy sady

Chopinova

Krkonošská

Church of the Most Sacred Heart of Our Lord

Legerova

Rubešova

Balbínova

Italská

Anny Letenské

13

11

Polská

Polská

Jiřího z Poděbrad

1

Růžová

VINOHRADY

Římská

18

Mánesova

Blanická

15

Třebízského

U Kanálky

19

náměstí Jiřího z Poděbrad

Škrétova

Anglická

5

Sázavská

Vinohradská

16

Slezská

Nitranská

7

IP Pavlova

Jugoslávská

Peace Square (náměstí Míru)

6

Náměstí Míru

Budečská

Korunní

U Vodárny

VINOHRADY

Rumunská

Moravská

Lublaňská

12

Bělehradská

Londýnská

Belgická

Americká

Varšavská

Francouzská

Lužická

Chodská

Slovenská

Koubkova

Zähřebská

Jana Masaryka

Máchova

Voroněžská

Rybalkova

Kozácká

Donská

Krymská

Wenzigova

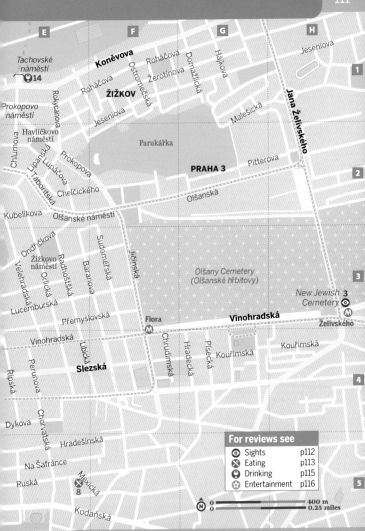

For reviews see

⊙ Sights	p112
✗ Eating	p113
🍷 Drinking	p115
✿ Entertainment	p116

400 m
0.25 miles

Sights

Church of the Most Sacred Heart of Our Lord

CHURCH

1 ◎ Map p110, D3

This church from 1932 is one of Prague's most original pieces of 20th-century architecture. It's the work of Jože Plečnik, a Slovenian architect who also worked on Prague Castle. The church is inspired by Egyptian temples and early Christian basilicas. It's usually only open to the public during mass. (Kostel Nejsvětějšího Srdce Páně; ☎ 222 727 713; www.srdcepane.cz; náměstí Jiřího z Poděbrad 19, Vinohrady; ⊙ services 8am & 6pm Mon-Sat, 9am, 11am & 6pm Sun; Ⓜ Jiřího z Poděbrad)

TV Tower

TOWER

2 ◎ Map p110, D3

Prague's tallest landmark – and depending on your tastes, either its ugliest or its most futuristic feature – is the 216m-tall TV Tower, erected between 1985 and 1992. But more bizarre than its architecture are the 10 giant crawling babies that appear to be exploring the outside of the tower – an installation called **Miminka** (Mummy; www.davidcerny.cz), by artist David Černý. (Televizní Vysílač; ☎ 210 320 081; www.tower park.cz; Mahlerovy sady 1, Žižkov; adult/child/family 200/120/490Kč; ⊙ observation decks 8am-midnight; Ⓜ Jiřího z Poděbrad)

New Jewish Cemetery

CEMETERY

3 ◎ Map p110, H3

Franz Kafka is buried in this cemetery, which opened around 1890 when the older Jewish cemetery – at the foot of the TV Tower – was closed. To find **Kafka's grave** (Ⓜ Želivského), follow the main avenue east (signposted), turn right at row 21, then left at the wall; it's at the end of the 'block'. Fans make a pilgrimage on 3 June, the anniversary of his death. (Nový židovské hřbitov; ☎ 226 235 216; www.kehilaprag.cz; Izraelská 1, Žižkov; admission free; ⊙ 9am-5pm Sun-Thu, to 2pm Fri Apr-Oct, 9am-4pm Sun-Thu, to 2pm Fri Nov-Mar, closed on Jewish holidays; Ⓜ Želivského)

Understand

How the Tower Got Its Babies

It was Czech artist-provacateur David Černý who first placed the creepy babies on the side of the Žižkov TV Tower in an installation called *Miminka* (Mummy), timed for Prague's reign as European Capital of Culture in 2000. The babies came down at the end of that year, but the resultant public outcry saw them reinstated, and it seems they're now a permanent fixture.

We're no art critics here, but the babies *are* sporting slotted faces, like a USB drive, lending at least one interpretation that the installation is intended as a commentary on our over-dependence on media for sustenance. Or maybe not. Come to think of it, the tower *does* look a bit like a baby's bottle...

National Monument

MUSEUM

4 Map p110, D1

While this monument's massive functionalist structure has all the elegance of a nuclear power station, the interior is a spectacular extravaganza of polished art-deco marble, gilt and mosaics, and is home to a fascinating museum of 20th-century Czechoslovak history. (Národní Památník na Vítkově; ☎224 497 600; www.nm.cz; U Památníku 1900, Žižkov; exhibition only adult/child 80/60Kč, roof terrace 80/50Kč, combined ticket 120/80Kč; ☉10am-6pm Wed-Sun Apr-Oct, Thu-Sun Nov-Mar; 🚌133, 175, 207)

Eating

Aromi

ITALIAN €€€

5 Map p110, B4

High ceilings, polished parquet floors and stylish, contemporary decor make this one of the city's prime venues to see and be seen. Aromi has a well-earned reputation for authentic, excellent Italian cuisine, at a price. The mood is brisk and businesslike at lunchtime, romantic in the evening. Advance booking essential. (☎222 713 222; www.aromi.cz; Náměstí Míru 6, Vinohrady; mains 400-600Kč; ☉noon-3pm & 5-11pm Mon-Sat, noon-10pm Sun; 🖥; MNáměstí Míru)

 Local Life

Riegrovy Sady

The hilltop **Riegrovy sady** (Rieger Gardens; entrance on Chopinova, across from Na Švihance, Vinohrady; ☉24hr; MJiřího z Poděbrad) gets press for its popular beer garden, but the green space itself is worthy of a visit. On the park's western side, a long grassy slope offers a magnificent view of Prague Castle and the city's red roofs. For a little peace and quiet, grab a beer or a sandwich from the beer garden (p109), or a smaller cafe in the park, and seat yourself on a wooden bench.

Vinohradský Parlament

CZECH €

6 Map p110, B4

This clean, bright and well-run pub features both a handsome early-modern, art-nouveau interior and a daring, inventive cooking staff who are willing to look beyond the standard pork and duck to other traditional Czech staples such as goose, rabbit and boar. Perfect for both lunch and dinner, but phone ahead to book a table as it's often jammed. (☎224 250 403; www.vinohradskyparlament. cz; Korunní 1, Vinohrady; mains 180-250Kč; ☉11am-midnight Mon-Wed, to 1am Thu-Sat, 11.30am-11.30pm Sun; 🖥; MNáměstí Míru)

Kofein
SPANISH €€

7 Map p110, D4

One of the hottest restaurants in town is this Spanish-style tapas place not far from the Jiřího z Poděbrad metro station. Descend into a lively space to see a red-faced chef minding the busy grill. Local faves include marinated trout with horseradish and pork belly confit with celeriac. Service is prompt and friendly. Book ahead. (273 132 145; www.ikofein.cz; Nitranská 9, Vinohrady; 3 tapas plates about 270Kč; 11am-midnight Mon-Fri, from 5pm Sat & Sun; M Jiřího z Poděbrad, 11, 13)

Understand
Not Big in Belgium

Design buffs beware. When Czechs talk about 'Brussels style', they're not referring to Belgian art nouveau or anything related to Henry Van de Velde. Rather, they're harking back to a heyday of their own national design when, despite the constraints of working under a communist regime, Czechoslovakia triumphed with its circular restaurant pavilion at the 1958 Brussels Expo. More than a hundred local designers took away awards, including porcelain designer Jaroslav Ježek, who won the Grand Prix for his Elka coffee service. The aesthetics of the time were similar to what you see at Café Kaaba. For a more authentic take, visit Veletržní Palác (p120).

Osteria Da Clara
ITALIAN €€

8 Map p110, E5

This minuscule Tuscan-style trattoria offers some of the most authentic and best-value Italian cooking in the city, though it will take a good map to find the place. The menu varies, but expect a handful of creative pasta dishes and main courses built around duck, beef, pork and seafood. Reserve in advance – there are only a few tables. (271 726 548; www.daclara.com; Mexická 7, Vršovice; mains 200-350Kč; 11am-3pm & 6-11pm Mon-Fri, noon-3.30pm & 6-11pm Sat, noon-4pm Sun; 4, 22)

The Tavern
BURGERS €

9 Map p110, C3

This cosy sit-down burger joint is the dream of a husband-and-wife team of American expats who wanted to create the perfect burger using organic products and free-range, grass-fed beef. Great pulled-pork sandwiches, fries and bourbon-based cocktails too. Reservations are taken (via the website) for dinner on Thursday, Friday and Saturday only. (www.eng. thetavern.cz; Chopinova 26, Vinohrady; burgers 140-200Kč; 11.30am-10pm Mon-Fri, brunch from 11am Sat & Sun; M Jiřího z Poděbrad, 11, 13)

Maso a Kobliha
GASTROPUB €

10 Map p110, B1

Established by the British chef at Sansho, across the street, this pub-style eatery (and butcher shop; the name means 'Meat and Doughnuts') serves hearty pub-style food prepared using locally grown, seasonal, organic produce – it's famous for its Scotch eggs, beef shin pies and freshly made doughnuts filled with vanilla cream. All-day brunch at weekends. (☎224 815 056; www.masoakobliha.cz; Petrská 23; mains 185-210Kč; � 9am-4pm Tue, to 10pm Wed-Fri, 10am-4pm Sat & Sun; ☎; ☐3, 8, 14, 24)

Pastička   CZECH €€

11 ✗ Map p110, B3

A warm, inviting ground-floor pub with a little garden out the back, Pastička is great for a beer or a meal. The interior design is part 1920s Prague and part Irish pub. Most come for the beer, but the mix of international and traditional Czech dishes is very good. (☎222 253 228; www.pasticka. cz; Blanická 25, Vinohrady; mains 150-330Kč; ☐11am-1am Mon-Fri, noon-midnight Sat; ☎; Ⓜ Jiřího z Poděbrad, ☐11, 13)

Drinking

Bio Zahrada   CAFE

12 ☕ Map p110, B5

This organic coffee shop serves high-end coffees and pastries in a welcoming, rustic setting with a big garden out back. Light food items are also served, including daily, good-value lunch specials like veggie curries and risottos, for around 130Kč. There's a small shop at the front that specialises in organic food items, including pastries, grains, dairy products and

TV Tower (p112)

tofu. (☎reservations 734 266 315; www. bio-zahrada.cz; Belgická 33, Vinohrady; ☐8.30am-9pm Mon-Thu, to 10pm Fri, 10am-8pm Sat; ☎; Ⓜ Náměstí Míru)

Café Kaaba   CAFE

13 ☕ Map p110, B3

Café Kaaba is a stylish little cafe-bar with retro furniture and pastel-coloured decor that comes straight out of the 1959 Ideal Homes Exhibition. It serves up excellent coffee made with freshly ground imported beans. Wi-fi is only free for customers from opening until 6pm. (☎reservations 222 254 021; www.kaaba.cz; Mánesova 20, Vinohrady;

Czech absinth

⏲8am-midnight Mon-Fri, from 9am Sat, from 10am Sun; 🛜; 🚊11, 13)

U Slovanské Lípy
PUB

14 🚇 Map p110, E1

A classic Žižkov pub, plain and unassuming in and out, 'At the Linden Trees' (the linden is a Czech and Slovak national emblem) is something of a place of pilgrimage for beer lovers. The reason is its range of artisan brews (from 28Kč for 0.5L), such as those from the Kocour brewery, including their superb Sumeček 11° (Catfish pale ale). (📞734 743 094; www. uslovanskelipy.cz; Tachovské náměstí 6, Žižkov; ⏲11am-midnight; 🛜🚻; 🚊133, 175, 207)

Saints
BAR

15 🚇 Map p110, C3

Sealing the deal on Prague's booming 'gay quarter' in Vinohrady, this British-run bar is laid-back, friendly and serves good drinks. With a multinational staff speaking many languages, it's the perfect entrée for newcomers to the local scene. (📞222 250 326; www.face book.com/thesaintsbar; Polská 32, Vinohrady; ⏲7pm-4am; Ⓜ Jiřího z Poděbrad)

Café Celebrity
CAFE

16 🚇 Map p110, B4

This cafe is part of the cluster of gay-friendly places that make up the old Radio Palác building. The Celebrity offers early-morning breakfasts on weekdays and a more relaxed brunch on weekends. At other times, it's great for coffee and people-watching. (📞222 511 343; www.celebritycafe.cz; Vinohradská 40, Vinohrady; ⏲8am-1am Mon-Fri, 5pm-2am Sat; 🛜; Ⓜ Náměstí Míru, 🚊11, 13)

Entertainment

Palác Akropolis
LIVE MUSIC

17 ⭐ Map p110, D2

The Akropolis is a Prague institution, a smoky, labyrinthine, sticky-floored shrine to alternative music and drama. Its various performance spaces host a smorgasbord of musical and cultural events, from DJs to string quartets to Macedonian Roma bands to local rock gods to visiting talent

Map p110

Understand
Absinth(e) Makes the Heart Grow Fonder

For many visitors, Prague is synonymous with absinth. That's been the case since the 1990s, when Czech drinks firm Hills cleverly revived this long-banned, legendary and allegedly hallucinatory 19th-century French-Swiss tipple. Today, however, the Swiss and French have resumed production of the genuine 'green fairy', and true connoisseurs hold their noses when it comes to replica 'Czechsinths'.

What's the difference? Most Czech brands (whether spelt absinth or absinthe) use oil to mix the active ingredient, wormwood, into the liquid, instead of properly distilling it. If you'll be packing a bottle in your suitcase, try the pricey but excellent Czech-made absinth *Toulouse Lautrec* (about 1200Kč at shops around town).

– Marianne Faithfull, the Flaming Lips and the Strokes have all played here. (📞 296 330 913; www.palacakropolis. cz; Kubelíkova 27, Žižkov; tickets free-250Kč; 🕑club 6.30pm-5am; 📶; 🚊5, 9, 15, 26)

Techtle Mechtle CLUB
18 ⭐ Map p110, B4

A popular cellar dance bar on Vinohrady's main drag. The name translates to 'hanky panky' in Czech, and that's what most of the swanky people who come here are after. In addition to a well-tended cocktail bar, you'll find a decent restaurant and dance floor, and occasional special events. Arrive early to get a good table. (📞 222 250 143; www.techtle-mechtle. cz; Vinohradská 47, Vinohrady; 🕑6pm-5am Tue-Sat; 📶; Ⓜ Náměstí Míru, 🚊11, 13)

Termix CLUB
19 ⭐ Map p110, C4

Termix is one of Prague's most popular gay dance clubs, with an industrial hi-tech vibe (lots of shiny steel, glass and plush sofas) and a young crowd that includes as many tourists as locals. The smallish dance floor fills up fast and you may have to queue to get in. (📞 222 710 462; www.club-termix.cz; Trebízského 4a, Vinohrady; 🕑9pm-6am Wed-Sun; Ⓜ Jiřího z Poděbrad, 🚊11, 13)

Explore

Holešovice

In Holešovice, you start to appreciate Prague as a genuine working city. Though sections of this former industrial quarter remain somewhat rundown, the neighbourhood has been slowly gentrifying. The hilltop beer garden at Letná is a relaxing spot on a warm evening in summer, while the National Gallery's impressive holdings at Veletržní Palác may be Prague's most underrated museum.

The Sights in a Day

☀ Start the morning with culture. If you're travelling with kids, head for the **National Technical Museum** (pictured left; p123), with its giant hall filled with historic locomotives and antique cars. If you're on your own, go for the eye-opening collection of modern art at the **Veletržní Palác** (p120). There are a lot of good cafes in the neighbourhood for a pick-me-up drink or some lunch – we like **Kumbal** (p126), just a short walk from the Veletržní Palác.

☀ After lunch, get some fresh air at one of the neighbourhood's two big parks: **Letná Gardens** (p123) or **Stromovka** (p124). The former has a handy beer garden, where an afternoon can easily slide into evening. Stromovka has more room to roam and is close to **Zoo Mořský Svět** (p123), the city's largest aquarium and another good spot for kids.

☾ Holešovice is short on good restaurants, but **Fraktal** (p126) has a killer burger and the Vietnamese at **Tràng An Restaurace** (p125) is worth the line up. Both are close to Letná Gardens. In the mood for a show? **Křižík's Fountain** (p124) pairs water gyrations with classical music. For clubbing, there's funky, postindustrial **Cross Club** (p126) or fashionable **Sasazu** (p127).

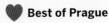

◉ Top Sights
Veletržní Palác (p120)

♥ Best of Prague

Bars & Pubs
Letná Beer Garden (p125)

Fraktal (p126)

Museums
Veletržní Palác (p120)

National Technical Museum (p123)

DOX Centre for Contemporary Art (p127)

For Kids
Stromovka (p124)

Zoo Mořský Svět (p123)

Nightlife
SaSaZu (p127)

Cross Club (p126)

Getting There

🚊 **Tram** Lines 1, 8, 12, 25, 26 to Letenské náměstí; lines 1, 6, 8, 12, 25, 26 to Strossmayerovo náměstí.

Ⓜ **Metro** Line C to Vltavská or Nádraží Holešovice.

Top Sights
Veletržní Palác

The National Gallery's collection of art from the 19th, 20th and 21st centuries is a must for serious art lovers, particularly fans of those modern movements – such as impressionism, constructivism, Dadaism and surrealism – that shattered the art world in the early 20th century. The holdings are strong on French impressionists, early modern masters like Schiele, Klimt and Picasso, and the talented generation of Czech artists working in the 1920s and '30s. Side exhibits look at trends in architecture and design.

Trade Fair Palace

Map p122, C3

www.ngprague.cz

Dukelských hrdinů 47

incl admission to all National Gallery venues, adult/child 300/150Kč

⊘10am-6pm Tue-Sun

M Vltavská, ⚊1, 6, 8, 12, 17, 25, 26

Veletržní Palác

French Collection

Thanks to a strong Bohemian interest in French painting, the palace's 3rd floor has an impressive collection of 19th- and 20th-century French art. Artists represented include Monet, Gauguin, Cézanne, Picasso, Delacroix and Rodin. Look for Gauguin's *Flight* and Van Gogh's *Green Wheat*.

Avant-Garde Czech Art

The museum's display of 20th-century Czech art (also on the 3rd floor) is one of the country's finest. Standouts include the geometric works by František Kupka, and cubist paintings, ceramics and design by several different artists – these paintings show an interesting parallel with the concurrent art scene in Paris. On the 2nd floor, look for the most contemporary Czech works across several genres.

Female Imagery in the International Collection

The 20th-century international collection, on the 1st floor, boasts works by some major names: Klimt, Schiele, Sherman and Miró, to name a few. Two highlights take on feminine themes: Klimt's luscious, vibrantly hued *The Virgins* and Schiele's much darker, foreboding *Pregnant Woman and Death*.

Alfons Mucha's Slav Epic

Until it goes on tour, the museum is also exhibiting Alfons Mucha's grandiose *Slav Epic (Slovanská Epopej)*, a collection of 20 giant paintings that tell the story of the Slavic peoples. Mucha dedicated much of his career to creating these canvasses. Entry requires a separate admission ticket.

☑ Top Tips

▶ The museum is huge. If you only have an hour or two, just hit the highlights listed here.

▶ If you're travelling with children, the museum offers a family pass for the discounted price of 350Kč.

▶ Pick up Prague postcards or souvenirs at the museum shop.

✗ Take a Break

The museum cafe, located on the ground floor and open during museum hours, is convenient for a coffee.

A few blocks away, the funky cafe Kumbal (p126) is a charming place for coffee or lunch.

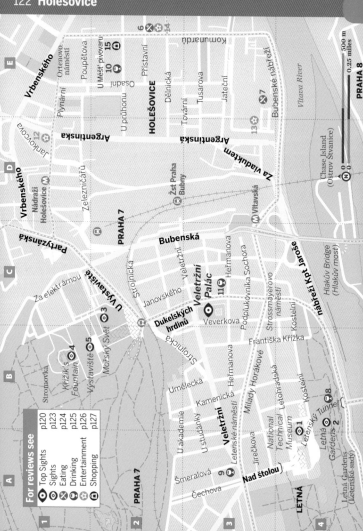

For reviews see

Top Sights		p120
Sights		p123
Eating		p124
Drinking		p125
Entertainment		p126
Shopping		p127

PRAHA 7

PRAHA 8

500 m
0.25 miles

Vltava River

Chase Island
(Ostrov Štvanice)

Hlávka Bridge
(Hlávkův most)

nábřeží Kpt Jaroše

Letenský Tunnel

Letná Gardens
(Letenské sady)

LETNÁ

National
Technical
Museum

Letná Gardens

Čechova

Šmeralova

Nad štolou

Jirečkova

Veletržní

Letenské náměstí

U akademie

U studánky

Kamenická

Umělecká

Milady Horákové

Letohradská

Kostelní

Kostelní

Strossmayerovo
náměstí

Františka Křížka

Veverkova

Heřmanova

Heřmanova

Podplukovníka Sochora

Veletržní
Palác

Bubenská

Veletržní

Janovského

Dukelských
hrdinů

Strojnická

Stojnická

U Výstaviště

Za elektrárnou

Stromovka

Křižík's
Fountain

Mořský Svět

Vystaviště

PRAHA 7

Železničářů

Nádraží
Holešovice

Vrbenského

Vrbenského

Partyzánská

Jankovcova

Plynární

Ortenovo
náměstí

Poupětova

U Měst pivovaru

Osadní

Přístavní

Dělnická

Tovární

Tusarova

Jateční

Za viaduktem

Argentinská

Argentinská

HOLEŠOVICE

U průhonu

Žst Praha
Bubny

Bubenské nábřeží

Vltavská

Komunardů

6 ⊗ ⊗ 14

10 15

12 ⊗

3 ⊙

4 ⊙

5 ⊙

1 ⊙

2 ⊙

8 ⊙

9 ⊙

11 ⊙

13 ⊗

7 ⊗

Sights

National Technical Museum

MUSEUM

1 Map p122, B4

Prague's most family-friendly museum got a high-tech renovation in 2012 and is a dazzling presentation of the country's industrial heritage. If that sounds dull, it's anything but. Start in the main hall, filled to the rafters with historic planes, trains and automobiles. There are separate halls devoted to exhibits on astronomy, photography, printing and architecture. (Národní Technické Muzeum; ☎220 399 111; www.ntm. cz; Kostelní 42; adult/concession 190/90Kč; ◷9am-5.30pm Tue-Fri, 10am-6pm Sat & Sun; 👶; ◻1, 8, 12, 25, 26 to Letenské náměstí)

Stromovka park (p124)

Letná Gardens

PARK

2 Map p122, B4

Lovely Letná Gardens occupies a bluff over the Vltava River, north of the Old Town, and has postcard-perfect views out over the city, river and bridges. It's ideal for walking, jogging and beer-drinking at a popular beer garden (p125) at the eastern end of the park. From the Old Town, find the entrance up a steep staircase at the northern end of Pařížská ulice. Alternatively, take the tram to Letenské náměstí and walk south for about 10 minutes. (Letenské sady; ◷24hr; 👶; ◻1, 8, 12, 25, 26 to Letenské náměstí)

Mořský Svět

AQUARIUM

3 Map p122, C2

The Czech 'Sea World' has the largest water tank in the country, with a capacity of around 100,000L. Some 4500 living species of fish and sea creatures are on display, with a good (and suitably scary) set of sharks. The cramped interior will be disappointing if you're used to larger marine-themed amusement parks around the world, though kids will certainly enjoy the experience. Special feeding shows and other special events are held through the week. See the website for details. (Sea World; ☎220 103 275, special events 736 649 558; www.morskysvet.cz; U Výstaviště

Local Life

Stromovka Park

Prague's largest central park, **Stromovka** (Královská obora; entry at Výstaviště or Nad Královskou oborou 21, Bubeneč; ⏱24hr; 🚊1, 8, 12, 25, 26), was once a medieval hunting ground for royals; now it's popular with strollers, joggers, cyclists and inline skaters. Kids can climb on the huge gnarled branches of ancient fallen trees or play at one of several playgrounds – and adults will appreciate the lavish tulip display in spring.

1, Bubeneč; adult/concession 280/180Kč; ⏱10am-7pm; ; 🚊12, 17)

Křižík's Fountain   FOUNTAIN

4 ◉ Map p122, B1

From spring to late autumn, the musical Křižík's Fountain performs its computer-controlled light-and-water dance, each evening. Performances range from classical music such as Dvořák's *New World Symphony* to rousing works performed by Andrea Bocelli, Queen or the Scorpions. Check the website for what's on. The show is best after sunset – from May to July go for later shows. (Křižíkova fontána; 📞723 665 694; www.krizikovafontana.cz; U Výstaviště 1, Bubeneč; 230Kč; ⏱performances hourly 7-11pm Mar-Nov; 👶; 🚊12, 17)

Výstaviště   CULTURAL CENTRE

5 ◉ Map p122, B1

This is a sprawling area of attractions and buildings of various architectural styles that was first laid out for the 1891 Jubilee Exhibition. These days it holds mainly trade fairs (see the website for a calendar), but also has a branch of the National Museum, a singing fountain (p124), the city's biggest aquarium (p123) and a slightly scruffy amusement park that's open daily from April to October. (Exhibition Grounds; 📞220 103 111; www.incheba.cz; Areál Výstaviště, Bubeneč; ⏱9am-11pm; 🚊12, 17)

Eating

Phill's Corner   INTERNATIONAL €

6 ✕ Map p122, E2

This tight, airy corner restaurant draws design inspiration from Holešovice's industrial past and its culinary cues from kitchens around the world, including Asia and the Middle East. The menu is well marked for food allergies, and there are ample gluten-free and other choices available. The daily lunch menu of soup and main course (around 150Kč) is a great deal. (📞731 836 988; www.facebook.com/phillscornercafe; Komunardů 32; mains 100-180Kč; ⏱7.30am-10pm Mon-Fri, 9am-6pm Sat & Sun; �📶; 🚊1, 6, 12, 14, 25)

MILKOVASA/SHUTTERSTOCK ©

Industrial Palace, Výstaviště

Tràng An Restaurace VIETNAMESE €

7 Map p122, E3

This low-key Vietnamese restaurant is the single best reason to trundle out to the sprawling **Holešovická tržnice** (Pražská tržnice, Prague Market; ✆ 220 800 592; www.holesovickatrznice.cz; Bubenské nábřeží 306; ⏰ 7am-6pm Mon-Fri, to 2pm Sat). Line up with everyone else at the counter and choose from a large picture menu on the wall. There's plenty of indoor seating and outside picnic tables in nice weather. Try to visit before or after typical meal times to avoid a wait. (✆ 220 560 041; www. facebook.com/asijskebistropodosmickou;

Bubenské nábřeží 306, Bldg 5, Holešovická tržnice/Pražská tržnice; mains 100-130Kč; ⏰ 9am-7pm Mon-Sat; 🚋 1, 12, 14, 25)

Drinking

Letná Beer Garden BEER GARDEN

8 🚇 Map p122, B4

No documenting of watering holes in the neighbourhood would be complete without a nod towards the city's best beer garden, with an amazing panorama, situated at the eastern end of the Letná Gardens (p123). Buy a takeaway beer from a small kiosk and grab a picnic table, or sit on a small terrace where you can order beer by the glass and decent pizza. (☑233 378 208; www.letenskyzamecek.cz; Letenské sady 341; ⏰11am-11pm May-Sep; 🚊1, 8, 12, 25, 26)

Fraktal
BAR

9 🚇 Map p122, A3

This subterranean space under a corner house near Letenské náměstí is easily the friendliest bar this side of the Vltava. This is especially true for English speakers, as Fraktal serves as a kind of unofficial expat watering hole. There's also good bar fare such as burgers (mains 120Kč to 300Kč). The only drawback is the early closing time (last orders at 11.30pm). (☑777 794 094; www.fraktalbar.cz; Šmeralová 1, Bubeneč; ⏰11am-midnight; 📶; 🚊1, 8, 12, 25, 26)

Local Life
Prague Zoo

Prague's attractive **zoo** (Zoo Praha; ☑296 112 230; www.zoopraha.cz; U Trojského zámku 120, Troja; adult/ concession/family 200/150/600Kč; ⏰9am-7pm Jun-Aug, to 6pm Apr, May, Sep & Oct, to 5pm Mar, to 4pm Nov-Feb; 👶; 🚊112, Ⓜ Nádraží Holešovice) is set on 60 hectares of wooded grounds on the banks of the Vltava. It makes for a great outing for kids. There are sizeable collections of giraffes and gorillas, but pride of place goes to a herd of rare horses. Attractions include a miniature cable car and a big play area.

Mecca
CLUB

10 🚇 Map p122, E2

This former warehouse in Holešovice boasts dancing on three floors (and five bars). It's only open sporadically, so check the website to check for parties and events during your stay. The music leans toward electronic and house, and the crowd tends to be a bit older – professionals in their 20s and 30s. (☑734 155 300; www.mecca.cz; U Průhonu 3; cover 100-200Kč; ⏰10pm-6am Fri & Sat; 📶; 🚊6, 12)

Kumbal
CAFE

11 🚇 Map p122, C3

This stylish coffee bar in a 1930s functionalist building manages to be both hip and comfortable at the same time. There's good coffee and tea, though not much on the menu apart from a few simple sandwiches and a daily soup (usually vegetarian). Breakfast is served every day until 11.30am. (☑604 959 323; www.kumbal.cz; Heřmanova 12; ⏰8am-9.30pm Mon-Fri, 9am-9.30pm Sat & Sun; 📶👶; 🚊1, 6, 8, 12, 17, 25, 26)

Entertainment

Cross Club
CLUB

12 ⭐ Map p122, D1

An industrial club in every sense of the word: the setting in an industrial zone; the thumping music (both DJs and live acts); and the interior, an absolute must-see jumble of gadgets, shafts, cranks and pipes, many of which move and pulsate with light to the music. The program includes occasional live music, theatre performances and art happenings. (☎736 535 010; www.crossclub.cz; Plynární 23; admission free-200Kč; ⊗cafe noon-2am, club 6pm-4am; 🛜; Ⓜ Nádraží Holešovice)

Sasazu

CLUB

13 ⭐ Map p122, D3

One of the most popular dance clubs in the city, Sasazu attracts the fashionable elite and hangers-on in equal measure. If you're into big dance floors and long lines (hint: go early), this is your place. Check the website for occasional big-name acts (such as Bastille or Morcheeba). Book a table in advance by phone (10am to 6pm Monday to Friday, 4pm to 10pm Saturday). (☎778 054 054; www.sasazu. com; Bubenské nábřeží 306, Hall 25, Pražská tržnice; admission 200-1000Kč; ⊗9pm-5am; 🛜; Ⓜ Vltavská, 🚊1, 12, 14, 25)

La Fabrika

THEATRE, PERFORMING ARTS

14 ⭐ Map p122, E2

The name refers to a 'factory', but this is actually a former paint warehouse that's been converted into an experimental performance space. Depending on the night, come here to catch live music (jazz or cabaret), theatre, dance or film. Consult the website for the latest program. Try to reserve in advance as shows typically sell out. (☎box office 774 417 644; www.lafabrika. cz; Komunardů 30; 200-400Kč; ⊗box office 2-7.30pm Mon-Fri; 🚊1, 6, 12, 14, 25)

Local Life

DOX Centre for Contemporary Art

Just a short tram ride away from Veletržní Palác, the **DOX Centre for Contemporary Art** (☎295 568 123; www.dox.cz; Poupětova 1; adult/ concession 180/90Kč; ⊗10am-6pm Mon, 11am-7pm Wed & Fri, 11am-9pm Thu, 10am-6pm Sat & Sun, closed Tue; 🚊6, 12 to Ortenovo náměstí) is a private gallery and museum that's trying to re-establish Holešovice's reputation as the repository of Prague's best modern art. This minimalist multilevel building occupies an entire corner block, providing Prague's most capacious gallery space, studded with a diverse range of thought-provoking contemporary art and photography. Don't miss DOX's excellent cafe and bookshop.

Shopping

Pivní Galerie

FOOD & DRINKS

15 🛍 Map p122, E2

If you think Czech beer begins and ends with Pilsner Urquell, a visit to the tasting room at Pivní Galerie (the Beer Gallery) will lift the scales from your eyes. Here you can sample and purchase a huge range of Bohemian and Moravian beers – nearly 150 varieties from 30 different breweries – with expert advice from the owners. (☎220 870 613; www.pivnigalerie.cz; U Průhonu 9; ⊗11.30am-7pm Mon-Fri; 🚊6, 12)

The Best of
Prague

Prague's Best Walks

Prague's Best...

View across Charles Bridge (p72)
KAPRIK/SHUTTERSTOCK ©

Best Walks
Kafka's Prague

🏃 The Walk

'This narrow circle encompasses my entire life', Franz Kafka (1883–1924) once said, drawing an outline around Prague's Old Town. While an exaggeration (he travelled and died abroad), Prague is a constant, unspoken presence in Kafka's writing, and this walk through the Old Town passes some of his regular haunts.

Start Náměstí Republiky; **M** Náměstí Republiky

Finish Hotel Intercontinental; **M** Staroměstská

Length 2km; 40 minutes

🍴 Take a Break

Near the Spanish Synagogue in Prague's old Jewish neighbourhood, **Bakeshop Praha** (p63) is a perfect corner spot for gourmet coffee and pastries.

House of the Minute

❶ Worker's Accident Insurance Company

Kafka's fiction was informed by his mundane day job as an insurance clerk; he worked for 14 years (1908–22) at the **Worker's Accident Insurance Company** at Na Poříčí 7. His walk home passed the **Powder Gate** (p75) and the newly built **Municipal House** (p75).

❷ House of the Three Kings

Just before the Old Town Sq at Celetná 3 is the **House of the Three Kings**, where the Kafkas lived from 1896 to 1907. Franz's room, overlooking the **Church of Our Lady Before Týn** (p71), is where he wrote his first story.

❸ Sixt House

Across Celetná, the **Sixt House** was an earlier childhood home (1888–89). Nearby, at Staroměstské náměstí 17, is **At the Unicorn** (U Jednorožce) – home to Berta Fanta, who hosted literary salons for thinkers of the day, including Kafka and a young Albert Einstein.

4 House of the Minute

The **House of the Minute** (dům U minuty), the Renaissance corner building attached to the Old Town Hall, was where Franz lived as a young boy (1889–96). He later recalled being dragged to his school in Masná street by the family cook.

5 Kafka's Birthplace

Just west of the **Church of St Nicholas** (p71) is **Kafka's birthplace**, marked by a bust of him at náměstí Franze Kafky

3 (formerly U Radnice 5). All that remains of the original house is the stone portal.

6 Kafka's Bachelor Pad

Despite several fraught love affairs, Kafka never married and lived mostly with his parents. One of his few **bachelor flats** can be found at Dlouhá 16.

7 Bílkova Apartment

Continuing north past the **Franz Kafka monument** (p62) you'll come to another of Kafka's

temporary **apartments** at Bílkova 22. In 1914 he began *The Trial* here.

8 Hotel Intercontinental

Head west to Pařížská and north towards the river. In the **Hotel Intercontinental's grounds** once stood another Kafka family apartment (1907–13), where Franz wrote his Oedipal short story 'The Judgment' (1912), and began *Metamorphosis,* about a man who transformed into a giant insect.

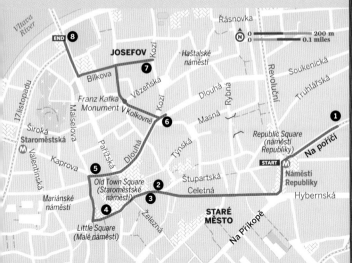

Best Walks
Velvet Revolution

🏃 The Walk

It's been almost 30 years since 1989's Velvet Revolution – when Czechs peacefully overthrew their communist overlords – but it will always be a landmark event. This walk takes you past the sites of the large-scale protests, strikes and press conferences that heralded epic change in the Czech Republic.

Start Národní třída; M Národní třída

Finish Former Radio Free Europe Building; M Muzeum

Length 2km; 45 minutes

🍴 Take a Break

Found just off Wenceslas Sq in a faded but formerly glamorous shopping gallery, **Kavárna Lucerna** (p87) is an atmospheric place for coffee or beer.

Museum of Communism (p90)

① Student Memorial

We start where the revolution itself began. The **bronze sculpture** under the arches marks the tragic events of 17 November 1989, when tens of thousands of students marching to remember Czechs murdered in WWII were attacked by riot police.

② Adria Palace

The beautiful, rondo-cubist **Adria Palace** (Národní třída 36) temporarily served as the headquarters of Civic Forum, the umbrella group formed by Václav Havel to represent the protesters and their demands. In the weeks after 17 November, this was a beehive of dissident activity.

③ Museum of Communism

The **Museum of Communism** (p90) illuminates local communist history – and the lies, privations and humiliations that ultimately drove the revolution demanding the regime's end. A short, graphic film shows the events of 1989.

❹ Melantrich Building

The action soon spread to nearby **Wenceslas Square** and the **Melantrich Building**, now a Marks & Spencer. On 24 November, Havel deposed 'Prague Spring' president Alexander Dubček addressed the crowds from its balcony.

❺ St Wenceslas Statue

The **Wenceslas Statue** (p87), at the upper end of the square, was bedecked by protesters with flags, posters and political slogans.

❻ Činoherní Klub Theatre

Prague's theatres were used for public discussions. The Civic Forum was formed on 19 November at **Činoherní Klub Theatre** (Ve Smečkách 26) and immediately demanded the resignations of communist functionaries.

❼ Jan Palach Memorial

Just in front of the **National Museum** is the **Jan Palach Memorial** (p87), an inlaid cross for a student who set himself on fire in 1969 to protest the Soviet-led Warsaw Pact invasion of the previous year – becoming a national hero in the process.

❽ Former Radio Free Europe Building

At the top of the square stands the former building for **Radio Free Europe** (p87), the US-funded radio station that helped bring down the communist regime. It now houses a branch of the National Museum.

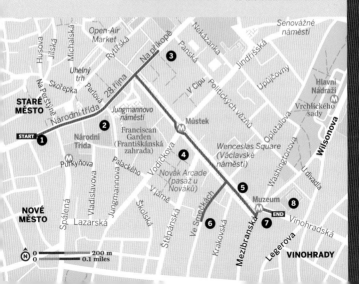

Best
Bars & Pubs

In the Czech Republic, drinking is a national pastime. It's no surprise, then, that Prague is an imbiber's playground. On practically every corner, there's another pub, wine bar, beer hall or cocktail lounge. Though it's traditionally a beer-drinker's city, the landscape is changing – a growing interest in national and international wines plus a trend towards classic cocktails are diversifying the scene.

MATT MUNRO/LONELY PLANET ©

Beer Basics

When it comes to beer *(pivo)*, Czechs prefer light lagers *(světlé)* to darker beers *(tmavé)*, though most pubs serve both. Pilsner Urquell is considered the best Czech brand, though Gambrinus, Budvar and Prague's own Staropramen are all popular. Czech beers are usually labelled either *dvanáctka* (12°) or *desítka* (10°) – but this doesn't refer to alcohol content (most beers are 4.5% to 5%). The 12° beers, like Pilsner Urquell, tend to be slightly heavier and stronger than 10° beers.

Microbrews & 'Tank' Beer

The global craft beer trend has reached the Czech Republic and is most pronounced in Prague, which boasts around a dozen brew pubs where DIY brewers proffer their own concoctions, usually accompanied by good traditional Czech cooking. To compete with the microbrews, the larger breweries have come up with several innovations, including offering unfiltered *(nefiltrované)* beer and hauling beer directly to pubs in supersized tanks (called, unsurprisingly, *tankové pivo*). Tank beer is said to be fresher than beer in traditional kegs, and that sounds good to us.

☑ **Top Tips**

▶ Pub tabs are usually recorded on a slip of paper on your table; don't write on it or lose it.

▶ You can usually order a beer in a pub without saying anything; when the waiter approaches, just raise your thumb for one beer, or thumb and index finger for two, etc.

▶ To pay up and go, say *zaplatím* (I'll pay).

▶ It's normal to tip a few crowns.

Cafe Louvre (p101)

Best for Beer

Prague Beer Museum Not a museum but a hugely popular pub, with 30 varieties on tap. (p64)

Jáma Rotating selection of regional beers and microbrews. (p92)

U Zlatého Tygra The classic Prague drinking den, where Václav Havel took Bill Clinton in 1994 to show him a real Czech pub. (p79)

Pivovarský Dům Popular microbrewery with several beers on tap and decent Czech food. (p101)

Letná Beer Garden A big beer garden with stunning views over Prague. (p125)

U Tří růží Tradition-reviving brewpub cooking up six different types of lager. (p78)

Best Cocktail Bars

Hemingway Bar Snug and sophisticated hideaway. (p80)

Hoffa Popular new bar, completely smoke free. (p92)

Bukowski's Dark and smoky expat cocktail dive. (p109)

Čili Bar Cute and compact, serves rum with chopped chilli peppers. (p80)

Tretter's New York Bar Upmarket New York–style cocktail bar. (p64)

Best for Wine

Le Caveau Cosy Vinohrady watering hole and deli features excellent French wine. (p109)

Café Kaaba Retro cafe with wines from around the world, sold by the glass. (p115)

Best Cafes

Grand Cafe Orient Stunning cubist gem with a sunny balcony. (p79)

Cafe Louvre Prague's most agreeable grand cafe and billiards hall. (p101)

Kavárna Obecní dům A legendary Viennese-style coffee house inside an art nouveau landmark. (p79)

Café Savoy Gorgeous coffee house with a lavish breakfast. (p48)

Cafe Kampus Student cafe that doubles as an art gallery and occasional music venue. (p80)

Best
Food

The restaurant scene in Prague gets better with each passing year. The latest trend is 'slow food' – traditional dishes given a refresh with locally sourced ingredients and less fat and starch. Recent years have seen an explosion in vegetarian and vegan restaurants, and international trends are strong as well.

Czech Cuisine

Czech food in Prague can be hit-and-miss. Traditional dishes like roast pork and sliced bread dumplings (*vepřová pečeně s knedlíky*) or roast beef in cream sauce (*svíčková na smetaně*) can be bland (as at many touristy restaurants in the centre) or memorable (when prepared by someone who cares) – choose your restaurants carefully. Other, often delicious, Czech staples include pork knuckle (*vepřové koleno*), duck (*kachna*) and goulash (*guláš*), here served with either beef or pork and bread dumplings.

International Foods

International food trends come and go with the same regularity as in other large cities. Alongside standard international cuisines like French and Italian – and especially pizza – Czechs have developed a taste for good Indian and Asian cooking as well as for steakhouses and Mexican food. The latest trends at the time of research include steakhouses, burgers and artisan food.

Vegetarian Options

The past few years have witnessed a revolution in healthy dining, with a growing number of vegetarian and vegan restaurants sprouting up around town. Alas, vegetarian options at traditional Czech restaurants seem to be as limited as ever, with the best bet

KOJIN/SHUTTERSTOCK ©

☑ Top Tips

▶ Some places charge a small *couvert* (to cover bread and condiments); this should be clearly marked on the menu.

▶ A 10% tip is customary but check to see it hasn't already been added to the bill.

▶ Avoid restaurants directly on Old Town Square and in the most heavily touristed zones – these are invariably mediocre.

being the ubiquitous (and often excellent) fried cheese (*smažený sýr*), served with a dollop of cranberry and/or tartar sauce.

Traditional Czech food

Best Fine Dining

V zátiší From high-end Indian cuisine to gourmet versions of traditional Czech dishes. (p78)

Kalina A little touch of Gallic sophistication in Staré Město. (p77)

Augustine Relaxed sophistication combined with the restaurant's own beer. (p48)

Best Czech Cuisine

Lokál Classic Czech dishes and great beer in a bright, modern beer hall. (p62)

Kolkovna A stylish, modern take on the traditional Prague pub. (p63)

Cafe Louvre Classic Czech cafe with surprisingly good homemade cooking. (p101)

Vinohradský Parlament A 21st-centruy take on the Czech pub. (p113)

Best for Vegetarians

Country Life Prague's first-ever health-food shop is an all-vegan cafeteria. (p78)

Lehká Hlava Exotic dining room with an emphasis on fresh preparation. (p78)

Maitrea Quality vegetarian and vegan cuisine amid unexpected designer decor. (p78)

Best for a Quick Lunch

Cukrkávalimonáda Achingly cute cafe with Renaissance-era painted roof beams. (p48)

Mistral Café Possibly the coolest bistro in the Old Town. (p64)

Bakeshop Praha A stylish bakery near the Jewish Quarter. (p63)

Best
Art

The city's holdings of fine art were pilfered over the centuries through wars and occupations, and museums here, while boasting occasional masterworks, lack the depth of galleries in Vienna and Paris. That said, the National Gallery's collections are strong in medieval art, baroque, and early modern surrealist and constructivist trends of the 20th century, when Czech artists came into their own.

The Underappreciated Alfons Mucha

Alfons Mucha (1860–1939) is probably the most famous visual artist to come out of the Czech lands, though because he attained his fame in Paris, and not in Prague, his reputation remains more exalted abroad than at home. Mucha is best known for his posters of French actress Sarah Bernhardt, but he was a prolific artist whose work is featured at St Vitus Cathedral (pictured above; p30) and the Municipal House (p75).

Best Art Museums

Veletržní Palác National Gallery's jaw-dropping collection of art from the 20th and 21st centuries. (p120)

Šternberg Palace National Gallery's collection of European art includes works by Goya and Rembrandt. (p36)

Mucha Museum Sensuous art nouveau posters, paintings and decorative panels of Alfons Mucha. (p89)

Convent of St Agnes Collection of medieval and early Renaissance art is a treasure house of glowing Gothic altar paintings. (p62)

Best Public Art

Miminka (Mummy) Ten creepy babies crawling atop the Žižkov TV Tower, by David Černý. (p112)

Proudy David Černý sculpture features two guys relieving themselves into a puddle shaped like the Czech Republic. (p43)

Franz Kafka Monument This unusual sculpture has a mini-Franz sitting piggyback on his own headless body. (p62)

Cubist Lamp Post The world's one and only. (p90)

Best
Museums

Prague has tons of museums, big and small, scattered around the city, and they make for great rainy-day options. Most museums cater to specific interests, but alas, many of the collections are of the old-school variety: static objects displayed behind thick glass. The recently refurbished, interactive and loads-of-fun National Technical Museum is a welcome exception and great for kids.

RUS S/SHUTTERSTOCK ©

Prague Jewish Museum
Displays the development of centuries of Jewish life and traditions with exhibitions in around half a dozen surviving synagogues. The highlight of the experience is to walk through the evocative former **Jewish cemetery**, with its thousands of jagged-edged tombstones. (p56; p58)

Karel Zeman Museum
Fascinating museum dedicated to a Czech film director who pioneered the art of special effects in movies. (p46)

National Technical Museum The Czech Republic's industrial heritage is on riotous display, with interactive exhibits and giant locomotives. (pictured above; p123)

Franz Kafka Museum
Hard-core fans will delight in the writer's original documents and photos. (p46)

Miniature Museum A delightfully quirky collection of miniature artwork, including the Lord's Prayer inscribed on a single strand of human hair. (p35)

Museum of Decorative Arts A feast for the eyes, full of 16th- to 19th-century artefacts, such as furniture, tapestries, porcelain and glass. (p61)

☑ Top Tips

▶ Austerity measures have forced museums to cut back on free-admission days and other price reductions, but many places still offer discounted family tickets.

▶ Most museums restrict photography or levy a painfully high fee for the privilege; flash photography is almost always banned.

▶ The **Prague City Card** (www.praguecitycard.com) offers free or discounted entry to around 50 sights, including many museums. Buy it at Prague City Tourism (p151) offices.

Best
History

RYHOR BRUYEU/GETTY IMAGES ©

Prague history reads like a long novel, chock full of characters who ride the city's fortunes from the heights of the Holy Roman Empire to the depths of the Eastern bloc (with chills and spills in between). Fortunately, the city was spared mass destruction in WWII, and it's all on full display. From the castle, to the churches, to the corner shop, every building has a story.

Best Royal Sights

Vyšehrad Citadel Where it all began – Prague's oldest fortification. (p104)

Prague Castle Seat of Czech power for a thousand years. (p24)

Astronomical Clock Ancient mechanical marvel that still chimes on the hour. (p71)

St Nicholas Church The height of Habsburg-inspired baroque splendour. (p45)

Best National Revivial

Municipal House Art nouveau apogee of art and national aspiration. (p75)

National Theatre Built to showcase emerging Czech music and drama. (p101)

Best for Modern History

National Memorial to the Heroes of the Heydrich Terror

Site where seven Czechoslovak partisans took refuge from the Nazis – and met tragic ends – in 1942. (p100)

TV Tower Communist power at its most potent. (p112)

John Lennon Wall This graffiti-splattered memorial was repainted each time the secret police whitewashed over it. (pictured above; p43)

Best
For Kids

Czechs are very family-oriented, so there are plenty of activities for children around the city. An increasing number of Prague restaurants cater specifically for children, with play areas and so on, and many offer a children's menu; even if they don't, they can usually provide smaller portions for a lower price.

NADEZDA MURMAKOVA/SHUTTERSTOCK ©

Into the Fresh Air

A great outing for kids (and parents) is Prague Zoo, located north of the centre in Troja. In addition, there are several other patches of green around town where you can spread a blanket and let the kids run free, such as Stromovka. Petřín is a beautiful park on a hill where parents and kids alike can take a break from sightseeing, and climb up the Petřín Lookout Tower for terrific views over Prague.

Best of the Outdoors

Stromovka Prague's largest central park, with lots of playgrounds. (p124)

Prague Zoo Aside from the animals, attractions include a miniature cable car. (pictured; p126)

Petřín Funicular Kids will get a thrill riding this funicular up to the top of the hill. (p41)

Slav Island Rent a paddle boat and enjoy a ride on the Vltava. (p99)

Best Indoor Activities

National Technical Museum A must-stop for inquisitive adolescents and their tech-savvy parents. (p123)

Miniature Museum Tiny exhibits and curiosities spark kids' imaginations at this delightful little museum. (p35)

☑ Top Tips

▶ Kids up to age 15 normally pay half-price for attractions (under 6 years free)

▶ On public transport, kids aged from six to 15 years pay half-price.

Laterna Magika Kids love the optical illusions onstage during the 'Black Light' theatre performances here. (p102)

Mořský Svět Prague's 'Sea World', at the Výstaviště exhibition grounds, boasts big aquariums and lots of aquatic life. (p123)

Best
For Free

Once a famously inexpensive destination, Prague is no longer cheap – there's not much on offer without a price attached. That said, in a city as beautiful as Prague, you don't need to spend lots of time (or money) on pricey museums. The parks and gardens, including the hilltop vista from Letná Gardens, are free, as is the street entertainment on Charles Bridge.

SOULOFBEACH/SHUTTERSTOCK ©

Prague Castle Without a Ticket

Admission to the interiors of Prague Castle, including St Vitus Cathedral, is hefty. But many people don't realize that the castle grounds, including the surrounding gardens, are free to roam at your leisure. The highlights of a visit here are the views over Malá Strana and the hourly changing of the guard; the most elaborate show is performed daily at noon.

Best Free Sights

Nový Svět Quarter
A delightful alternative to Prague Castle's Golden Lane. (p36)

Petřín Hill Entrance to the park is gratis; skip the funicular and just hike up. (p40)

Astronomical Clock
The hourly chiming is public and free. (p71)

Vyšehrad Cemetery
The beautiful cemetery is the final resting place for composers Smetana and Dvořák, as well as art nouveau artist Alfons Mucha. (pictured; p105)

Letná Gardens The sweeping views are free; beers from the beer garden cost extra. (p123)

☑ Top Tips

▶ Ask at tourist-information offices about free concerts, theatrical performances and cultural events happening during your visit.

▶ Visits to most churches (except St Vitus Cathedral and St Nicholas Church in Malá Strana) are free.

▶ Although you'll have to pay for a guided tour of the Municipal House (p75), you can wander through the glorious art nouveau cafe and to the downstairs American Bar without a ticket.

Best
Architecture

Prague is an open-air museum of architecture; most of the centre is protected as a Unesco World Heritage listing. Prague's architectural heritage was built up over the centuries, with the earliest buildings in the Romanesque and Gothic styles dating back nearly a thousand years. Later styles like Renaissance, baroque, neoclassical, art nouveau and modern were added over time as fashions changed.

Best Romanesque & Gothic

Rotunda of St Martin Tiny, circular church in Vyšehrad is reputedly Prague's oldest standing building and a perfect example of Romanesque architecture. (p105)

St Vitus Cathedral Gothic to the tips of its famous spires. (p30)

Charles Bridge Prague's most famous bridge is a Gothic landmark. (p72)

Best Renaissance & Baroque

St Nicholas Church In Malá Strana, the mother of all baroque churches in Prague. (p45)

Loreta The pilgrimage site is modelled after the Italian original. (p32)

Best National Revival & Art Nouveau

Municipal House Glittering art nouveau in top form. (p75)

Grand Hotel Evropa Fading grandeur at this ornate art nouveau hotel and cafe. (pictured; p87)

Best Modern Architecture

Dancing Building The shape of the building mimics a dancing couple. (p99)

ANTONS/SHUTTERSTOCK/SHUTTERSTOCK ©

☑ **Top Tips**

▶ For more on Prague architecture, take a specialised tour such as Thousand Years of Prague Architecture (www.walkingtours.cz).

▶ *Prague: An Architectural Guide* is a photographic encyclopaedia by Mark Smith, Michal Schonberg and Radomira Sedlakova.

Veletržní Palác This mammoth functionalist structure from the 1920s doesn't look like your everyday palace. (p120)

Best
Shopping

Although the streets are lined with stores, Prague doesn't initially seem a particularly inspiring shopping destination. But if you know where to look, you can find above-average versions of classic Czech souvenirs: Bohemian crystal and glassware, garnet and amber jewellery, and wooden marionettes. Think outside the box: Czech liquor, farm-produced beauty products and old-school children's toys all make great gifts.

For mainstream shopping, central Na Příkopě boasts international chains from H&M to Zara. For the most part, you can put your wallet away along Wenceslas Sq (not a bad idea anyway, considering the pickpocketing that goes on here). Instead, explore the Old Town's winding alleyways. Ritzy Pařížská is often called Prague's Champs Élysées and is lined with luxury brands like Cartier, Dolce & Gabbana, Hugo Boss and Ferragamo. Dlouhá, Dušní and surrounding streets house some original fashion boutiques, while even central Celetná contains a worthwhile stop or two.

Best for Unique Souvenirs

Botanicus Rustic-chic beauty products from this popular old apothecary. (p83)

Manufaktura Specialises in Czech traditional crafts and wooden toys. (pictured; p83)

Art Deco Galerie Czech antiques galore; hunt for treasures here on a rainy day. (p83)

Best for Design & Glass

Modernista Czech cubist and art deco design with cool ceramics, jewellery, posters and books. (p83)

Moser Ornate Bohemian glass objects. (p95)

Artěl Traditional glass-making meets modern design in this stylish shop in Malá Strana. (p51)

Best for Books & Toys

Marionety Truhlář In Malá Strana, quirky shop stocks traditional marionettes from workshops around the Czech Republic. (p51)

Shakespeare & Sons More than just a bookshop – a congenial literary hang-out. (p51)

Houpací Kůň The Rocking Horse Toy Shop has high-quality, traditional Czech toys. (p37)

Survival Guide

Survival Guide

Before You Go

When to Go

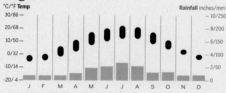

Prague
°C/°F Temp
Rainfall inches/mm

→ Spring (Apr–Jun)
April is the start of the tourist season. Trees bud in mid-April. Accommodation tightens at Easter and for the Prague Spring music festival in May.

→ Summer (Jul–Aug)
Sunny and occasionally hot. All attractions open.

→ Autumn (Sep–Oct)
Often sunny but cool. Some attractions close on 1 October for winter.

→ Winter (Nov–Mar)
Short, dark days, snow and occasionally blustery winds. Tourists descend for lively Christmas and New Year festivities.

Book Your Stay

→ Air-conditioning isn't necessary most of the year.

→ Parking can be very tight. If driving, work out parking details with the hotel in advance and avoid hotels in Malá Strana and the Old Town.

→ Many private singles or doubles in hostels are very nice and offer excellent value.

→ You can often find last-minute bargains for the top-end hotels on the standard online booking sites.

→ Malá Strana is a particularly scenic location in which to stay, but it's worth considering a room in one of Prague's inner suburbs like Vinohrady, Smíchov or Holešovice, as central Prague is easily reached by public transport.

Useful Websites

Hotels Prague Listings of the city's best historic hotels and B&Bs.

Guide Prague Well-run booking site that offers plenty of photos.

Booking.com Helps you make reservations at hundreds of Prague hotels.

Lonely Planet Author-recommended reviews and online booking.

Best Budget

Fusion Hotel (📞226 222 800; www.fusionhotels.com; Panská 9; r from 2650Kč; @🛜; 🚊3, 5, 6, 9, 14, 24) It's a hostel, it's a hotel, it's a designer heaven...

Holiday Home (📞222 512 710; www.holidayhome. cz; Americká 37, Vinohrady; s/d from 1200/1400Kč; P😊@🛜; MNáměstí Míru) Popular, family-owned pension in a quiet neighbourhood.

Mosaic House (📞221 595 350; www.mosaichouse. com; Odborů 4; dm/tw from 370/2400Kč; 😊✳@🛜; 🚊5) A blend of four-star hotel and boutique hostel with designer details.

Czech Inn (📞reception 267 267 612, reservations 267 267 600; www.czech-inn.com; Francouzská 76, Vršovice; dm

280-450Kč, s/d 1200/1600Kč, apt from 3000Kč; P😊@🛜; 🚊4, 22) Great value and atmosphere in an up-and-coming neighbourhood.

Best Midrange

Domus Henrici (📞220 511 369; www.domus-henrici. cz; Loretánská 11; s/d/ste 3150/3600/4400Kč; @🛜; 🚊22) Peaceful seclusion just a short stroll from the castle.

Lokál Inn (📞257 014 800; www.lokalinn.cz; Míšeňská 12; d/ste from 3800/4600Kč; 😊🛜; 🚊12, 15, 20, 22) Lovely baroque setting with excellent restaurant close to Charles Bridge.

Hunger Wall Residence (📞257 404 040; www.hunger wall.eu; Plaská 8; 2-person apt from 3100Kč; 😊🛜; 🚊9, 12, 15, 20) Spotlessly clean and modernised short-stay apartments.

Dům u velké boty (📞257 532 088; www.dumuvelkeboty. cz; Vlašská 30; s/d from 2160/2850Kč; 😊🛜; 🚊12, 15, 20, 22) Lovely old pension set on a quiet square.

Best Top End

Golden Well (📞257 011 213; www.goldenwell. cz; U Zlaté studně 4; d/

ste from 4750/14,900Kč; P😊✳@🛜; MMalostran-ská, 🚊12, 15, 20, 22) Hotel Historic, luxury hotel in the ultimate location – beneath the castle walls.

Savic Hotel (📞224 248 555; www.savic.eu; Jilská 7; r from 4800Kč; ✳@🛜; MMůstek) Housed in a former monastery, this hotel is bursting with character.

Icon Hotel (📞221 634 100; www.iconhotel.eu; V Jámě 6; r from 3800Kč; ✳@🛜; 🚊3, 5, 6, 9, 14, 24) Cutting-edge designer hotel that's a hang-out for Prague's beautiful people.

Le Palais (📞234 634 111; www.lepalaishotel.eu; U Zvonařky 1, Vinohrady; r from €180, ste from €280; P😊✳@🛜; 🚊6, 11, 13) Luxury hotel housed in a gorgeous belle époque building.

Best Short-Stay Apartments

Happy House Rentals (📞224 947 623; www.happy houserentals.com; Uruguay-ská 12, Vinohrady; 🕐9am-6pm Mon-Fri; MNáměstí Míru) Specialises in short- and long-term rental apartments.

Mary's Travel & Tourist Service (☎222 253 511; www.marys.cz; Anny Letenské 17, Vinohrady; ☺9am-7pm Mon-Fri, 10am-5pm Sat & Sun; Ⓜ Jiřího z Poděbrad, ☒11, 13) Friendly agency offering private rooms, hostels, pensions, apartments and hotels in Prague and surrounding areas.

Prague Apartments (☎604 168 756; www.prague-apartment.com) Web-based service with comfortable, Ikea-furnished flats. Availability of apartments shown online.

Stop City (☎222 521 233; www.stopcity.com; Belgická 36, Vinohrady; ☺10am-8pm; Ⓜ Náměstí Míru) Specialises in apartments, private rooms and pensions in the city centre, Vinohrady and Žižkov areas.

Arriving in Prague

Václav Havel Airport Prague

This international airport is 17km west of the city centre.

➡ **Airport Express (AE) Bus** Runs between the airport and Prague's main

train station at 30-minute intervals. Service starts at 5am and the last bus leaves around 9.30pm. Buy 60Kč tickets from the driver.

➡ **AAA Radio Taxi** (www.aaataxi.cz) Prague's most reliable taxi service. A ride to náměstí Republiky costs about 600Kč.

➡ **Bus 119.** This city bus terminates at the closest metro station, Nádraží Veleslavín (Line A). The whole trip to the centre is 32/16Kč per adult/concession. A luggage tickets costs an extra 16Kč.

Prague Main Train Station

Nearly all international trains arrive at Prague's main station, **Praha hlavní nádraží** (Prague Main Train Station; ☎840 112 113; www.cd.cz; Wilsonova 8, Nové Město; ☺3.30am-12.30am; Ⓜ Hlavní nádraží), connected to the rest of the city by metro Line C.

Note that some trains arrive at Prague's other large train station, **Praha-Holešovice** (Nádraží Holešovice; ☎840 112 113; www.cd.cz; Vrbenského, Holešovice; Ⓜ Nádraží Holešovice), conveniently connected to the Nádraží Holešovice station on metro Line C.

Florenc Bus Station

Almost all international buses use **Florenc bus station** (ÚAN Praha Florenc; ☎900 144 444; www.florenc.cz; Křižíkova 2110/2b, Karlín; ☺5am-midnight; ☎; Ⓜ Florenc), accessible by both the metro's B and C lines.

Getting Around

Prague has an excellent integrated public-transport system (www.dpp.cz) of metro, trams, buses and night trams, but when you're moving around the compact Old Town or the castle area, it will be more convenient – and scenic – to use your feet. Times between tram stops are posted at each stop and on www.dpp.cz.

Metro

☑ **Best for...** Quick transportation between major sights, connecting to the train station and venturing outside the tourist areas.

➡ The metro operates from 5am to midnight.

➡ There are three lines: Line A (green) runs from Nemocnice Motol in the west to Depo Hostivař in the east; Line B (yellow) runs from Zličín in the southwest to Černý Most in the northeast; and Line C (red) runs from Háje in the southeast to Letňany in the north.

➧ Services are fast and frequent. The nearest metro station is noted after the m in listings.

➧ You must buy a ticket (*jízdenka*) before boarding, and then validate it by punching it in the little yellow machine in the metro-station lobby or on the bus or tram when you begin your journey. Checks by inspectors are frequent.

➧ You'll need coins for ticket machines at metro stations and major tram stops. You can also buy tickets at news-stands, some hotels, tourist-information offices and metro-station ticket offices. Some machines can now handle contactless cards, but your foreign bank will charge you a hefty fee for the pleasure of paying this way.

Tram & Bus

☑ **Best for**... Scenic rides, connecting to attractions far off the metro lines, and for travellers

Tickets & Passes

Tickets are interchangeable on all metros, trams and buses. Buy tickets at metro stations or nearby news-stands – but never from the driver. If you're staying longer than a few hours, it's easier to buy a one-day or three-day pass.

Basic ticket Valid for 90 minutes; adult/concession 32/16Kč

Short-term ticket Valid for 30 minutes; adult/concession 24/12Kč

One-day ticket Valid for 24 hours; adult/concession 110/55Kč

Three-day ticket Valid for 72 hours; 310Kč for all ages

who can't easily walk from point A to B. Most visitors won't have any reason to get on a bus, but a tram ride is a classic Prague experience.

➧ Important tram lines to remember are 22 (runs to Prague Castle, Malá Strana and Charles Bridge), 17 and 18 (run to the Jewish Quarter and Old Town Sq) and 11 (runs to Žižkov and Vinohrady).

➧ Regular tram and bus services operate from 5am to midnight (see www.dpp.cz for maps and timetables). After this, night trams (91 to 99) and buses (901 to 915) take over.

➧ All night trams intersect at Lazarská in Nové Město.

➧ Be aware that few tram or bus stops sell tickets. So if you're using single tickets, buy several in the metro station or at newspaper stands, then save a couple of unstamped ones for later and validate them upon boarding.

Taxi

☑ **Best for**... Late-night rides back to the hotel, airport transfers, and when you're running late for a show or performance.

➧ Prague's taxis are known for scams. If a driver won't switch on the meter, find another taxi.

→ Look for the 'Taxi Fair Place' scheme, which provides authorised taxis in key tourist areas. Drivers can charge a maximum fare and must announce the estimated price in advance.

→ Within the city centre, trips should be around 150Kč to 200Kč, a trip to the suburbs no more than 450Kč, and to the airport from around 600Kč to 700Kč.
The following radio-taxi services are reliable and honest:

AAA Radio Taxi (☏14014, 222 333 222; www.aaataxi.cz)

Halo Taxi (☏244 114 411; www.halotaxi.cz)

ProfiTaxi (☏14015; www.profitaxi.cz)

Essential Information

Business Hours

Banks 8am to 4.30pm Monday to Friday

Bars 11am to midnight or later

Main post office (Jindřišská 14, Nové Město) 2am to midnight

Shops 8.30am to 8pm Monday to Friday, to 6pm Saturday and Sunday

Restaurants 10am to 11pm, though kitchens often close by 10pm

Electricity

**Type E
220V/50Hz**

Money

→ Credit cards are widely accepted.

→ The Czech crown (Koruna česká, or Kč) is divided into 100 hellers

(h), though these tiny coins no longer circulate. Prices are sometimes denominated in fractions of crowns. In these instances, the total is rounded to the nearest whole crown.

→ Keep small change handy for public toilets and tram-ticket machines.

Safe Travel

Prague is a low-crime city and safer than most Western cities. Pickpocketing and petty theft, however, remain rife, especially around the main tourist attractions. If you are the victim of a pickpocket, report the crime as soon as possible at any nearby police station. Remember to retain any paperwork you might need for insurance purposes.

For lost or stolen passports, embassies can normally issue travel documents swiftly.

Toilets

Public toilets are free in state-run museums,

Tipping

The general advice on tipping is to round up the bill in restaurants, bars and taxis to the nearest 50Kč or 100Kč. This is what Czechs do.

Money-Saving Tips

➡ Forget taxis – take a shuttle bus from the airport to the city, then walk or use public transport.

➡ Skip the sushi and eat Czech food; you'll find the best value for your crowns in pubs. Look for set-lunch specials.

➡ Local beer is much cheaper than wine (and delicious).

➡ Don't exchange cash at the airport. Instead, withdraw local currency with your ATM card.

➡ Don't worry about missing museums if cash is tight – Prague is best explored outdoors and on foot.

➡ When going to the theatre, you can get cheaper tickets for around 200Kč.

galleries and concert halls. Elsewhere, such as at train, bus and metro stations, public toilets charge around 10Kč. Men's are marked *muži* or *páni,* and women's *ženy* or *dámy.*

Tourist Information

Prague City Tourism offices are good sources of maps and general information, as well as an excellent resource for finding what's on. The website (www.prague.eu) is in English.

Prague City Tourism – Airport (Prague Welcome; ☎221 714 714; www.prague. eu; Terminals 1 & 2, Václav Havel Airport Prague, Ruzyně; ⏰8am-8pm; ☒100, 119)

Prague City Tourism – Rytírská (Prague Welcome;

Map p74; ☎221 714 444; www.prague.eu; Rytírská 12, Staré Město; ⏰9am-7pm; Ⓜ Můstek)

Prague City Tourism – Old Town Hall (Prague Welcome; Map p74; ☎221 714 714; www.prague. eu; Staroměstské náměstí 5, Old Town Hall; ⏰9am-7pm; Ⓜ Staroměstská)

Travellers with Disabilities

Prague and the Czech Republic are behind the curve when it comes to catering to travellers with disabilities. One exception is the Prague Public Transport Authority which is making all stations wheelchair-friendly. See www.dpp.cz for details.

➡ **Prague Wheelchair Users Organisation**
(Pražská organizace vozíčkářů; Map p60; ☎224 826 078; www.pov.cz; Benediktská 6; ⏰9am-4pm Mon-Thu, to 3pm Fri; Ⓜ Náměstí Republiky) Works to promote barrier-free architecture and improve the lives of people with disablities. Consult the website for online resources.

➡ **Czech Blind United**
(Sjednocená Organizace Nevidomých a Slabozrakých v ČR; Map p98; ☎221 462 462; www.sons.cz; Krakovská 21, Nové Město; ⏰9am-noon & 2-4.30pm Mon; Ⓜ Muzeum) Represents the vision-impaired; provides information but no services.

Language

Czech belongs to the western branch of the Slavic language family. Many travellers flinch when they see written Czech, but pronouncing it is not as hard as it may seem at first. Most of the sounds in Czech are also found in English, and of the few that aren't, only one can be a little tricky to master – *rzh* (written as *ř*). Also, Czech letters always have the same pronunciation, so you'll become familiar with their pronunciation really quickly.

With a little practice and reading our pronunciation guides as if they were English, you'll be understood. Just make sure you always stress the first syllable of a word – in italics in this chapter – and pronounce any vowel written with an accent mark over it as a long sound. In this chapter (m/f) indicates masculine and feminine forms.

To enhance your trip with a phrasebook, visit **lonelyplanet.com**. Lonely Planet iPhone phrasebooks are available through the Apple App store.

Basics

Hello.
Ahoj.   *uh*·hoy

Goodbye.
Na shledanou.   *nuh*·skhle·duh·noh

Excuse me.
Promiňte.   *pro*·min'·te

Sorry.
Promiňte.   *pro*·min'·te

Please.
Prosím.   *pro*·seem

Thank you.
Děkuji.   *dye*·ku·yi

Yes./No.
Ano./Ne.   *uh*·no/ne

Do you speak English?
Mluvíte   *mlu*·vee·te
anglicky?   *uhn*·glits·ki

I don't understand.
Nerozumím.   *ne*·ro·zu·meem

Eating & Drinking

I'm a vegetarian. (m/f)
Jsem vegetarián/   *ysem* ve·ge·tuh·ri·an/
vegetariánka.   ve·ge·tuh·ri·an·ka

Cheers!
Na zdraví!   nuh *zdruh*·vee

That was delicious!
To bylo lahodné!   to *bi*·lo *luh*·hod·nair

Please bring the bill.
Prosím   *pro*·seem
přineste účet.   *przhi*·nes·te oo·chet

I'd like ... , please. (m/f)
Chtěl/Chtěla   khtyel/*khtye*·luh
bych ..., prosím.   bikh ... *pro*·seem

a table for (two)	*stůl pro (dva)*	stool pro (dvuh)
that dish	*ten pokrm*	ten *po*·krm
the drinks list	*nápojový lístek*	*na*·po·yo·vee lees·tek

Shopping

I'm looking for ...
Hledám ...   *hle*·dam ...

How much is it?
Kolik to stojí?   *ko*·lik to *sto*·yee

That's too expensive.
To je moc drahé.   to ye mots *druh*·hair

Can you lower the price?
Můžete mi   moo·zhe·te mi
snížit cenu?   snyee·zhit tse·nu

Emergencies

Help!
Pomoc!   po·mots

Call a doctor!
Zavolejte   zuh·vo·ley·te
lékaře!   lair·kuh·rzhe

Call the police!
Zavolejte   zuh·vo·ley·te
policii!   po·li·tsi·yi

I'm lost. (m/f)
Zabloudil/   zuh·bloh·dyil/
Zabloudila   zuh·bloh·dyi·luh
jsem.   ysem

I'm ill. (m/f)
Jsem nemocný/   ysem ne·mots·nee/
nemocná.   ne·mots·na

Where are the toilets?
Kde jsou toalety?   gde ysoh to·uh·le·ti

Time & Numbers

What time is it?
Kolik je hodin?   ko·lik ye ho·dyin

It's (10) o'clock.
Je jedna   ye yed·nuh
hodina.   ho·dyi·nuh

At what time?
V kolik hodin?   f ko·lik ho·dyin

morning	*ráno*	ra·no
afternoon	*odpoledne*	ot·po·led·ne
evening	*večer*	ve·cher
yesterday	*včera*	fche·ruh
today	*dnes*	dnes
tomorrow	*zítra*	zee·truh

1	*jeden*	ye·den
2	*dva*	dvuh
3	*tři*	trzhi
4	*čtyři*	chti·rzhi
5	*pět*	pyet
6	*šest*	shest
7	*sedm*	se·dm
8	*osm*	o·sm
9	*devět*	de·vyet
10	*deset*	de·set

Transport & Directions

Where's the ...?
Kde je ...?   gde ye ...

What's the address?
Jaká je   yuh·ka ye
adresa?   uh·dre·suh

Can you show me (on the map)?
Můžete   moo·zhe·te
mi to ukázat   mi to u·ka·zuht
(na mapě)?   (nuh muh·pye)

A ticket to ..., please.
Jízdenku   yeez·den·ku
do ..., prosim.   do ... pro·seem

What time does the bus/train leave?
V kolik hodin   f ko·lik ho·dyin
odjíždí   od·yeezh·dyee
autobus/vlak?   ow·to·bus/vluhk

Please stop here.
Prosím vás   pro·seem vas
zastavte.   zuhs·tuhf·te

I'd like a taxi.
Potřebuji   po·trzhe·bu·yi
taxíka.   tuhk·see·kuh

Is this taxi available?
Je tento taxík   ye ten·to tuhk·seek
volný?   vol·nee

Behind the Scenes

Send Us Your Feedback

We love to hear from travellers – your comments help make our books better. We read every word, and we guarantee that your feedback goes straight to the authors. Visit **lonelyplanet.com/contact** to submit your updates and suggestions.

Note: We may edit, reproduce and incorporate your comments in Lonely Planet products such as guidebooks, websites and digital products, so let us know if you don't want your comments reproduced or your name acknowledged. For a copy of our privacy policy visit lonelyplanet.com/privacy.

Our Readers

Many thanks to Ahliddin Gaffar and Roderick Henderson who wrote to us with useful advice and andecdotes.

Mark's Thanks

Thanks to my editors at Lonely Planet, my co-author Neil Wilson and lots of people on the ground in my adopted city of Prague. These include: Kateřina Pavlitová at prague.eu; Irena Dudová, Zuzi and Jan Valenta at tasteofprague.com; Iva Roze Skochová, Petr Kučera and 'Karim' at pragulic.cz, and many more.

Neil's Thanks

Many thanks go to Jan Valenta at taste ofprague.com; Bogdan and Irina; Alena Volpakova; Kraig and Lisa; Carol; and my co-researcher, Mark Baker.

Acknowledgements

Cover photograph: Charles Bridge, Prague, Pietro Canali /4Corners©

Contents photograph: Charles Bridge, Prague, Pyty/Shutterstock©

This Book

This 5th edition of Lonely Planet's *Pocket Prague* guidebook was curated by Marc Di Duca and researched and written by Mark Baker and Neil Wilson. The previous edition was written by Mark Baker.

This guidebook was produced by the following:

Destination Editor
Gemma Graham

Product Editor Anne Mason

Senior Cartographer
David Kemp

Book Designer
Gwen Cotter

Assisting Editors Will Allen, Victoria Harrison, Gabrielle Innes, Gabrielle Stefanos

Cover Researcher
Naomi Parker

Thanks to Liz Abbott, Shona Gray, Katherine Marsh, Jenna Myers, Susan Paterson, Lyahna Spencer, Tony Wheeler

Index

✕ Eating

◉ Drinking

Our Writers

Marc Di Duca

A travel author for the last decade, Marc has worked for Lonely Planet in Siberia, Slovakia, Bavaria, England, Ukraine, Austria, Poland, Croatia, Portugal, Madeira and on the Trans-Siberian Railway, as well as writing and updating tens of other guides for other publishers. When not on the road, Marc lives between Sandwich, Kent and Mariánské Lázně in the Czech Republic with his wife and two sons.

Mark Baker

Mark is a freelance travel writer with a penchant for offbeat stories and forgotten places. He's originally from the United States, but now makes his home in the Czech capital, Prague. He writes mainly on Eastern and Central Europe for Lonely Planet as well as other leading travel publishers, but finds real satisfaction in digging up stories in places that are too remote or quirky for the guides. Mark is on Twitter @markbakerprague and Instagram @markbakerprague

Neil Wilson

Neil was born in Scotland and has lived there most of his life. Based in Perthshire, he has been a full-time writer since 1988, working on more than 80 guidebooks for various publishers, including the Lonely Planet guides to Scotland, England, Ireland and Prague. An outdoors enthusiast since childhood, Neil is an active hill-walker, mountain-biker, sailor, snowboarder, fly-fisher and rock-climber, and has climbed and tramped in four continents.

Published by Lonely Planet Global Limited
CRN 554153
5th edition – Nov 2017
ISBN 978 1 78657 157 1
© Lonely Planet 2017   Photographs © as indicated 2017
10 9 8 7 6 5 4 3 2 1
Printed in China